A Body Across the Map

Artists and Issues in the Theatre

August W. Staub
General Editor

Vol. 11

PETER LANG
New York • Washington, D.C./Baltimore • Boston • Bern
Frankfurt am Main • Berlin • Brussels • Vienna • Canterbury

Michael Taav

A Body Across the Map

The Father-Son Plays of Sam Shepard

PETER LANG
New York • Washington, D.C./Baltimore • Boston • Bern
Frankfurt am Main • Berlin • Brussels • Vienna • Canterbury

Library of Congress Cataloging-in-Publication Data

Taav, Michael.
A body across the map: the father-son plays of Sam Shepard / Michael Taav.
p. cm. — (Artists and issues in the theatre; vol. 11)
Includes bibliographical references (p.   ).
1. Shepard, Sam. 1943–   —Criticism and interpretation.
2. Fathers and sons in literature. I. Title. II. Series.
PS3569.H394Z895   812'.54—dc21   98-46182
ISBN 0-8204-4433-2
ISSN 1051-9718

Die Deutsche Bibliothek-CIP-Einheitsaufnahme

Taav, Michael:
A body across the map: the father-son plays of Sam Shepard / Michael Taav.
–New York; Washington, D.C./Baltimore; Boston; Bern;
Frankfurt am Main; Berlin; Brussels; Vienna; Canterbury: Lang.
(Artists and issues in the theatre; Vol. 11)
ISBN 0-8204-4433-2

Cover design by Nona Reuter
Author photograph by Jim Thorne

The paper in this book meets the guidelines for permanence and durability
of the Committee on Production Guidelines for Book Longevity
of the Council of Library Resources.

© 2000 Peter Lang Publishing, Inc., New York

All rights reserved.
Reprint or reproduction, even partially, in all forms such as microfilm,
xerography, microfiche, microcard, and offset strictly prohibited.

Printed in the United States of America

Acknowledgment

I wish to thank Professor Stanley Waren for his long-standing support and guidance. I am also grateful to Professors Daniel Gerould, Miriam D'Aponte, and Harry Carlson for their insights and recommendations. Lastly, I wish to express my appreciation to my beloved parents and Tracy Stewart Granger for their love and encouragement.

Contents

Chapter One	Introduction	1
Chapter Two	*The Rock Garden* and *The Holy Ghostly*: A Boy's Eye View	5
Chapter Three	*The Tooth of Crime*: The Worm Turns	15
Chapter Four	*Curse of the Starving Class*: Biology (Alas) Is Destiny	33
Chapter Five	*Buried Child*; Buried Children	49
Chapter Six	*True West*: The Spell of the Hermit King	65
Chapter Seven	*A Lie of the Mind*: The Curse's End	79
Chapter Eight	Conclusion	107
Bibliography		113

Chapter One

Introduction

Sam Shepard's plays have long interested me. I recall first being introduced to his work in 1973 when a friend gave me a badly xeroxed copy of *The Tooth of Crime*. The play had a very profound impact. It was not that the work was thematically unique; plays dealing with the dangers inherent in both American success and failure, in the commercialization of our best impulses, have long been a part of our theatre. Rather, it was Shepard's characters and their idioms which clearly distinguished his work from that of both his contemporaries and the major American playwrights who had preceded him. Shepard was truly a rock-and-roller, a man who, either by inclination or lack of choice, had taken for his banner the whole, coarse, colorful fabric of American popular culture. Here was a playwright who was writing about his generation from the inside, who shared its enthusiasm for beatnik cool, science fiction, gangster films, and rock-and-roll, and was able to take these disparate forms, filter them through a poetic imagination and create serious art.

Since that epiphanic introduction, I have followed Shepard's work closely, taking careful note of how it has (and has not) evolved in terms of structure, characterization, theme, and central conflict. I first perceived Shepard's plays to deal primarily with a social order in conflict; be it with an emerging counterculture, or its own mythic and idealized past. As I continued to study his work, however, I began to discern that beneath this conflict often lies a more archetypal struggle, that between fathers and sons. It is my contention, in fact, that it is this conflict which dominates a major part of Shepard's work and that if investigated chronologically, one will be able to see clearly how Shepard's moral perspective has not only reversed itself through time but has grown more complex and profound.

Furthermore, I believe that there exists a central dramatic action common to all the father-son plays. Each work focusses upon the son's attempt to extricate himself both physically and psycho-spiritually from his father or father surrogate. In Shepard's earlier plays, *The Rock Garden*, *The Holy Ghostly*, and *The Tooth of Crime*, the "sons" succeed in breaking free by defeating the "fathers" via a competition of some sort. In the family plays, *Curse of the Starving Class* and *Buried Child*, the sons fail in their attempts at autonomy, and instead fall prey to the same hereditary curses which befell their fathers. In *True West*, it is the hermit father, via his surrogate, who defeats the son, punishing him for having dared to create an independent life. In *A Lie of the Mind*, Shepard utilizes elements from many of the earlier father-son plays, creating a drama where the protagonist both falls victim to a father's curse *and* destroys him. What distinguishes this, Shepard's most hopeful work, from his earlier ones, is that the son suffers for what he has done, and as a result is spiritually transformed. Initially violent and self-deceiving, he emerges from the play gentle and contrite, having transcended his father's curse.

While Shepard's work continues to call forth an ever-increasing array of critical responses, many of which discuss plays which will be analyzed in my text, none, with the exception of Henry Schvey's essay, "A Worm in the Wood: The Father-Son Relationship in the Plays of Sam Shepard,"[1] has yet singularly focussed on the father-son conflict that I believe is central to so much of his work. In fact, if this conflict is touched upon at all, it is done only in passing, as one thematic concern among many.

In the ensuing chapters, father-son conflict will be investigated chronologically, beginning with *The Rock Garden* and concluding with *A Lie of the Mind*. Each conflict will be analyzed in terms of the qualities ascribed the fathers and sons, the issues they debate, and the manner in which their conflicts are waged and resolved. Furthermore, beginning with *Curse of the Starving Class* and continuing through *Buried Child* to *A Lie of The Mind*, this conflict will be studied not in singular terms, as merely a battle between two individuals, but in the context of the family as a whole. In these, the family plays, the father-son conflict will be examined in regards to how it affects and is affected by other familial conflicts, namely those between husband and wife, mother and son, and (in the cases of *Curse of the Starving Class* and *A Lie of the Mind*) brother and sister. With the exception of *True West*, I shall only examine those plays where the antagonists are either actual fathers and sons (*The Holy Ghostly, Curse of the Starving Class, Buried Child, A Lie of the Mind*) or figurative ones (*The Rock Garden, The Tooth of Crime*). *True West* will also be included for although the antagonists are brothers, Lee has so allied himself with his absent father that he serves, in large part, as his surrogate and champion.

Notes

1 *Modern Drama*, 36, (March 1993), 12–25.

Chapter Two

The Rock Garden and *The Holy Ghostly*: A Boy's Eye View

The Rock Garden, a ten-page, one-act play, written in 1964 while Shepard was in his very early twenties, portrays the Oedipal conflict in an oblique, almost lackadaisical manner and without the rancor which characterizes much of his subsequent work. Rather than have the figurative father and son directly attack each other verbally or physically, Shepard simply places them in close proximity to one another, allows each to give voice to his governing obsessions, and in so doing reveals both the huge psycho-spiritual gulf dividing them and the "son's" essential superiority.

What most conspicuously separates the son and father figures are their attitudes towards sex. Whereas Boy is obsessed with sex—he thinks about it in the first scene, and graphically describes it in the third—Man's libido has diminished to the point of invisibility. Whether motivated by fear, revulsion, apathy, or some strange mix of the three, he nonetheless sidesteps whatever sexual invitations are made him. The clearest indication of just how far Man has fallen, sexually speaking, is when he finds his wife/lover waiting for him naked in bed. Rather than respond to this obvious sexual opportunity, Man behaves as if he had happened upon a convalescing stranger; he takes a seat at some distance from her, makes a brief, half-hearted attempt to say, at least, something, and that done, sinks back into silence.

(HE [MAN] crosses to the rocking chair and sits. For a long while the MAN just sits rocking. The WOMAN [in bed] stares at the ceiling.)

MAN   Kind of drafty.
WOMAN Yes.
MAN   Must be the windows.

WOMAN I guess so.

(A long silence while the MAN rocks. The lights dim slowly.)[1]

Having exhausted whatever socio-sexual energy he once had, Man now directs his attention, with a comic singularity that borders on the pathological, towards improving home and property. In the play's final scene, he outlines what is left of his worldly ambition:

> If we can get the fence painted by next week . . . we could have some nice [rock] gardens like the one I have now. Only bigger and more fancy. . . . We could put a fountain in ours . . . take care of the orchard . . . [and] put some of them [aluminum pipes] in.[2]

What's most striking about Man's plans is his choice of a rock garden as the locus for all his energies and intentions. At first glance, it seems incongruous for a middle-class, middle-aged homeowner in some unnamed American suburb to obsess over something so exotic and so rich in foreign religious associations, until one discovers that for Man, unlike his Zen Buddhist counterparts, a rock garden has no spiritual, metaphysical, or even much aesthetic significance; it is simply a species of middle-class busy work, a safe, solitary, and respectable way for a bourgeois male to kill time, and simultaneously avoid the social and sexual demands of marriage. In Man we see a Sisyphus who is actually happy with his fate, who prefers pushing the same few rocks around day after day to anything as dangerously unpredictable as a human exchange. That Shepard opposes such preferences, and, in fact, thinks them utterly ridiculous, is made clear by the manner in which he has Man express himself:

> The lawn here is different you know. This one is different from the other one. . . . It's harder to get to. The other one didn't have as many sprinkler heads as this. The other one didn't have any, did it? No, the other one was easy. I remember the other one.[3]

With his preoccupation with the mundane, and his predilection for stating and restating the obvious, Man shows himself to have all the imaginative inflexibility of a Bergsonian buffoon.[4]

Boy, on the other hand, demonstrates no such "inelasticity."[5] When he does finally speak at length he continually presents new information, and is constantly embellishing and building upon what he's already said. His behavior is similarly expansive. Rather than try to reduce experience to a small number of fixed actions directed towards an almost pitifully insignificant end, Boy's focus is outward, beyond the solitary self.[6] Driven by his own sexuality, and newly discovered sexual prowess, Boy has entered a wider world—the same world from which Man has fled—where the self is not something to be withdrawn, but offered up, where all action is a form of generosity, and where pleasure, if it truly be pleasure, must be shared:

> I like going down on girls, too. . . . She gives me some head and then I give her some. Just sort of a give-and-take thing. . . . There's different ways. . . . Actually girls really like fingers almost as well as a penis you know? If you move your fingers fast enough they'd rather have it that way almost.[7]

In the play's third and final scene, Shepard brings the "son" and "father" figures together for what in retrospect is a most uncharacteristically benign showdown where the point is not to destroy one another but rather to demonstrate philosophical superiority. And the fact that Boy wins this contest so easily and so inadvertently (his monologue is more a private revery than a conscious rebuttal)[8] is indicative of just how insubstantial Man's value system really is. Hidden amongst his rocks, Man may have found a temporary haven, but when forced out into the open, when made to acknowledge the existence of an alternative and more vital way of living, he, and by extension his belief system, is immediately sent sprawling.

Considering that *The Rock Garden* was written in the early sixties, when the youth culture was first beginning to define itself as something vaguely inimical and apart, and when Shepard himself was all of twenty-one, it should come as no surprise that the play would show each generation as not only distinct from, but antithetical to the other. At a time when one's allegiances were in large part determined by when one was born, it was not uncommon for the young (or, for that matter, the not-so-young) to give themselves over to melodramatic generalization, to see themselves as spiritual and sexual utopians, while viewing their elders essentially as flag-wavers for the unenlightenment—blighted souls consumed by material obsession and sexual terror.

Shepard's next father-son play, *The Holy Ghostly*, is similarly a reflection of its particular time. Written in 1968, by which time the peaceful self-assertions of "tuning in and dropping out" had given way to the actual waging of generational war, it is a far angrier, far more polemical work—and yet in the end, a far more ambivalent work—than *The Rock Garden*. In this play, the father figure, Pop, and his son, Ice, stand in undisguised ideological opposition to one another. Each, in his way, feels fundamentally short-changed by the other and it is this sense of having been betrayed by someone who knows one best, and ideally should love one the most, which pushes Pop and Ice past mere belligerence to renunciation, and finally to murder.

Like Man, his counterpart in *The Rock Garden*, Pop is a middle-aged materialist who is forced in defeat to admit the existence of an alternative reality far greater and more encompassing than his own. Where the two fathers differ most notably, however, is in how they choose to deal with this reality; for whereas Man flees the great world beyond by burying himself amongst his rocks, Pop actively seeks it out, intending to do battle, destroy it, and reassert the primacy of his own material reality.

It becomes quickly apparent, however, that Pop has overreached himself, that he is as much fool as he is hero, with neither the percipience nor the weaponry for a fight of this magnitude. Courageous enough to do battle with the Otherworld, as represented by the Chindi, an Indian daemon, he is nonetheless sufficiently ridiculous to think he can defeat it with a few rifles and some hand-made artillery. Pop is like a cowboy Quixote—or to be more precise, a Quixote reversed; for while Cervantes's hero mistakes windmills for monstrous giants, Pop, in his naive arrogance, looks upon monstrous giants and sees only windmills. This, in fact, is Pop's great flaw: he is so inextricably bound to the physical world, and so devoid of any real spiritual understanding, that he perceives the supernatural world as some aberrant extension of his own world rather than as something distinct and unfathomable with the power to intrude omnipotently.

In his own way, and despite his capacity for what Richard Gilman terms "ignoble heroics,"[9] Pop shows that, like Man in *The Rock Garden*, he too is an ostrich of sorts, burying his head in the sands of an earthly reality in a pitiable attempt to protect himself from the greater realities surrounding him.

Eventually though, after his war strategies (such as they are) prove useless, Pop's eyes are opened to the actuality of his situation and his courage gives way to fear. Pop is so utterly diminished, in fact, by his new self-knowledge that he forfeits his claim to authority of any sort; henceforth he will be the child who seeks solace from his son, and Ice, the father who consoles.

    POP Ice, could you tell me a story? I feel lonely.
    ICE Sure. Turn the radio off and come on over here.

(POP turns the radio off and crawls over to ICE and curls up in his lap. ICE strokes his forehead and tells him a story. . . .)

ICE Once upon a time millions and millions of years ago, before man was ever around, there was a huge fiery ball of fire.
POP Like the sun?
ICE Sort of—but much huger and hotter than our sun. A super sun. At the same time, somewhere in space there was a giant planet made out of cosmic ice.
POP What's cosmic mean?
ICE Of, or pertaining to, the cosmos.
POP What's the cosmos?
ICE Everything.[10]

Implicit in this exchange of identities is an alternative view of adulthood. Rather than hold to the conventional notion of age and earthly experience as the determinants of maturity, Shepard defines true adulthood as a consequence of cosmological insight. The authentic adult does not concern himself with his few belongings, his earthly name, trivial belittlings of those around him, or for that matter with all that "bullshit about . . . hard work and guts and never say die."[11] Rather he allies himself with the World Beyond, and is therefore able to look at earthy concerns and earthly realities from a perspective so broad as to distinguish what is of true human importance, and what is mere narcissistic desperation.

In contrast with *The Rock Garden*, *The Holy Ghostly* does not conclude with this exchange of identities, with the son supplanting the father. It is not enough for Ice, as it was for Boy, simply to ascend to the throne that his father has surrendered; he must disassociate himself from Pop altogether.[12] Having begun this process of repudiation previous to the play's action by changing his name to Ice and moving to New York, he now continues it by reappearing on-stage in the white war paint of the Chindi.[13] It is this realliance, this disavowal of his biological father in favor of a spiritual one, that allows Ice to at last go through his ultimate rite of passage.

This rite begins with a diatribe, a symbolic patricide, in which Ice finally denounces Pop as a "pathetic creep" who treated him like a "slave."[14] This denunciation, however, has little effect on the older man; he still clings to the notion of a future where together he and Ice will "set . . . [the] world on fire", if only Ice would "go down by the crick and wash that damn make-up off . . . [his] face."[15] It is Pop's intractability, his refusal to acknowledge Ice as anything more than a manifestation of himself, that leads Ice ever farther from his father, and ever closer to the ultimate act of disaffiliation until finally, when Pop asks to be paid back for "some time once when you needed me and I helped you,"[16] Ice—without a moment's hesitation—whips out his pistol and shoots him.

Admittedly, it is difficult to know precisely what to make of this, the play's climactic moment, for it is neither preceded by any discernible character crisis nor followed by a denouement. In fact what makes this patricide all the more shocking is that it happens so suddenly, is performed so casually, and that in its wake, Ice, rather than offering up some insight as to his motives, vanishes from the play altogether.[17] This leaves the audience the uncomfortable task of trying to ascribe a motive when none was clearly given. Is this shooting simply the final hard-hearted manifestation of some unexpressed hurt or is it something more benevolent? Could it be that Ice is, in fact, "helping" his father; that he now knows, having had a spiritual awakening, that by shooting Pop he will finally release his father from what Ernest Becker calls "the colossal burden of the self-dominating, self-forming life?"[18] Or on the other hand, is it, strictly speaking, not a murder at all, but simply the final means available of proving to Pop what the Chindi and his consort, the White Witch, seem to have known from the outset; namely, that he is already "a ghost . . . who has died without ever finishing what he had to do on the earth"?[19]

Adding to the puzzle is the fact that Shepard never addresses what Pop has done specifically to merit his fate. Unlike, say, Weston in *Curse of the Starving Class*, he has not abandoned his family. Nor has he, like Dodge in *Buried Child*, committed some terrible crime. In fact, when Pop does soliloquize, what he recalls is not some past sin or familial catastrophe but his utter exultation at his son's birth.

> I was feelin alright 'cause about that time I got myself something to look forward to stateside. I'm comin' home to my little woman in Rapid City, South Dakota, and she's got one hell of a package waiting fer me. She's got me a son, a son with my name and my eyes and my nose and my mouth. My own flesh and blood, boy. My son, Stanley Hewitt Moss the seventh.[20]

Furthermore, if one looks back at Ice's diatribe in search of concrete evidence, what one finds, rather than a chronicle of horrific abuse, is the standard stuff of adolescent complaint: too many chores, cliched advice, and a parent "who just doesn't get it".

> For eighteen years I was your slave. I worked for you hand and foot. Shearing the sheep, irrigating the trees, listening to your bullshit about "improve your mind, you'll never get ahead, learn how to lose, hard work and guts and never say die". . . .[21]

Consequently, by denying Ice a large enough provocation for his actions, Shepard has suddenly (and might one dare suggest, unwittingly) reversed the play's moral position. Defined from the very outset as *The Holy Ghostly*'s right-thinking *raisonneur*, Ice now appears to be, as a result of this unjustified shooting, not a seeker of justice but, as his name suggests, a cold, hard, often querulous sociopath. Similarly, Pop, who throughout the play has been declared "wrong" by his son, the Chindi, and his consort, the White Witch, is now perceived as more sinned against than sinner, more victim than victimizer.

It is this sudden reversal of sympathy that transforms *The Holy Ghostly* from a simple-minded polemic chronicling the easy triumph of a spiritually enlightened son over his materialistic father into something more ambivalent and peculiar: a polemic that inadvertently recoils from its own insistence. For the fact is, that at the play's end, our sympathies lie with Pop, that "fucking mess . . . strung out between right and wrong, good and evil . . . the right and the left, the high and the low,"[22] who despite his spiritual myopia and philistine values truly loves his son, and not with Ice who—though embraced by the Spirit World and blessed with certain cosmological insights—behaves at his moment of liberation[23] with all the spite and fury of a surly fifteen-year-old on a first drunk.

Notes

1. Sam Shepard, *The Rock Garden in Angel City, Curse of the Starving Class & Other Plays*, Preface by Jack Gelber (New York: Urizen Books, 1976), 222.

2. Ibid., 218.

3. Ibid., 222–223.

4. Henri Bergson defines the comic as "that side of a person which reveals his likeness to a thing, that aspect of human events which, through its peculiar inelasticity conveys the impression of pure mechanism, or automatism." (117) It is repetition, the "following up on . . . one idea, and continually recurring to it"(180) to the exclusion of all else, that characterizes Shepard's Man as one of Bergson's comic automatons *in Laughter, in Comedy*, introduction by Wylie Sypher. (Garden City, NY: Doubleday, 1956)

5. Ibid., 117.

6. Martin Tucker, however, appears to discount Boy's view of sex as reciprocity, as an active exchange of pleasures with another, arguing that at play's end, Boy still remains "in a womb of self-centeredness." *Sam Shepard* (New York: Continuum, 1992), 29.

7. *Rock Garden*, 226.

8. Ron Mottram decribes Boy's final monologue as "an aggressive response to all that is no longer bearable in the boy's home life." *Inner Landscapes: The Theatre of Sam Shepard* (Columbia: University of Missouri Press, 1984), 12. Yet, when one considers that this speech is delivered matter-of-factly and not in direct response to anything Man has said, it becomes difficult to look upon it as a conscious attack. If anything, it, in revealing Boy's contrasting preoccupations, might be looked upon as an unconscious display of passive-aggression.

9. *Faith, Sex, Mystery* (New York: Simon and Schuster, 1986), 85.

10. Sam Shepard, *The Holy Ghostly*, in *The Unseen Hand and Other Plays* (New York: Bobbs-Merrill, 1972), 105–107.

11. Ibid., 97.

12. According to Doris Auerbach, *The Holy Ghostly* deals with the reordering of the familial hierarchy, with the "son returning to confront the father and wrest power from him." See "Who Was Icarus's Mother?" *Rereading Shepard*, ed. Leonard Wilcox (New York: Garland, 1988), 56. This description, however, seems more applicable to *The Tooth of Crime* than this play. Rather than subordinate his father and rule in his stead, Ice seeks to forge an identity that

is antithetical to the one Pop bequeathed him. He is motivated not by the need to dominate (as he himself was dominated) but by the need to exist autonomously.

13 *The Holy Ghostly*, 95.

14 Ibid., 97.

15 Ibid., 108.

16 Ibid., 109.

17 Conversely, Martin Tucker sees this patricide as comically dramatized and hence there is "no shock of horror . . . in the commission of it." *Sam Shepard* (New York: Continuum, 1992), 68. It is my contention, however, that the act itself is indeed shocking both in the context of the events which preceded it and the manner in which it is realized, and that this shock is only mitigated later by Pop's response.

18 *The Denial of Death* (New York: The Free Press, 1973), 116.

19 *Holy Ghostly*, 100.

20 Ibid., 95.

21 However murky Ice's motives, what is clear is that Pop, once shot, is spiritually transformed. It is in fact, one of the play's more obvious ironies that Pop, ever the empiricist, can only embrace the spirit world once he himself has become a spirit. And while there is clearly something comic about the now dead Pop dancing about and declaring himself "a changed man . . . [who] never felt more alive," (111) the play nonetheless ends on a note of sincere spiritual celebration as Pop euphorically renounces his old values by first throwing his material possessions and then his own body/corpse into the fire.

22 *Holy Ghostly*, 101–102.

23 It need be reiterated that by shooting Pop, Ice does finally break free from his father's psycho-spiritual grasp. He achieves his autonomy, albeit (as noted earlier) in a manner which in some measure discredits him.

Chapter Three

The Tooth of Crime: The Worm Turns

The Tooth of Crime, first published and performed in 1972, is, within the context of Shepard's canon, a most singular achievement. Not only is it considered by some critics his most linguistically inventive[1] and, as Richard Gilman[2] and Stanley Kauffmann[3] have pointed out, most structurally cohesive play; it is also, when compared, at least, to his earlier father-son plays, his most pessimistic.[4] In *The Rock Garden* and *The Holy Ghostly* the victories of Boy and Ice, respectively, represent if not "good" winning out over "evil," then at least "right" winning out over "wrong" and by extension suggest an essentially optimistic world view. In *The Tooth of Crime*, however, the triumph of the young Gypsy marker, Crow, over the older, more successful Hoss portends no such optimism; rather, it prophesies a harsh Darwinian future where the less encumbered an individual is by moral codes, the more he personifies a pure will to power, the greater his chances for success.

Concomitant with Shepard's darkening world view is an equally radical realignment of his sympathies. In *The Tooth of Crime* we see Shepard—for the first time—siding unequivocally with the defeated father figure rather than with the triumphant "son."[5] This does not mean, however, that this shift in allegiance has produced any corresponding shift in values, that Shepard has suddenly renounced his earlier recantations and re-embraced the class to which he was born. Quite the contrary. What he has done, in the character of Hoss, is create a father figure whose circumstance is, generally speaking, identifiable with his own: namely, that of a cultural outlaw who, having long waged war against caution and respectability, having long flown "in the eye of [mass] contempt,"[6] now discovers himself on the brink of mass acceptance.

With his entrance at the beginning of Act One onto a stage empty except for his "evil-looking black"[7] throne, Hoss, dressed in "black rocker gear with silver studs and black kid gloves,"[8] is immediately announced as an unconventional father figure, far more dangerous and powerful than those in *The Rock Garden* and *The Holy Ghostly*.[9] We soon learn, in fact, that he is the preeminent "marker" (i.e., a killer/participant) in the Game, a futuristic competition which exemplifies Marcuse's dictum that "in this society everything can be coopted, everything can be digested."[10] Drawing upon the varied iconography of American deviance (i.e., the rock-and-roller, the Mafioso, the gunslinger, the drag racer), the Game's "Keepers" have created a pop-cultural entertainment wherein the combatants—under a rigidly enforced rule system, and in exchange for territory, points, huge prizes, and if sufficiently successful, pop-cultural immortality—wage war to the death.

Despite his success, or perhaps because of it, Hoss's relationship both to the Game and the world beyond it has grown increasingly uncertain. The quintessential "solo marker" who always stood and fought alone, Hoss has long believed in both the idea of autonomous individuality and an attendant moral order in which one's actions serve as the sole determinants of one's fate. Now, however, Hoss finds his autonomy inhibited not only by the demands of his own success but, even more significantly, by a new and comparatively capricious *Zeitgeist*. As he makes clear in his introductory song/prologue, "The Way Things Are,"[11] the Judeo-Christian universe of personal accountability, of "an eye for an eye" (be it in the here-and-now and/or the hereafter), has suddenly been superceded by one where, lamentably, "everybody's doin' time for everybody else's crime."[12] Now it is the phenomenological manifestations of some vast psychohistorical Gestalt that decide individual destiny rather than the individual himself. Hence, "the heroes,"[13] traditionally, the triumphant standard-bearers of an individuated moral order, "are dyin' like flies,"[14] extinguished en masse by forces utterly irresponsive to their courage and skill. Indeed, from Hoss's standpoint, this new universe appears so nihilistic as to have dispensed with moral arbitration altogether, utilizing instead a type of cosmic lottery in which virtue and vice go unacknowledged, rewards and punishments are meted out arbitrarily, and which so disconnects Man from both his immediate and ultimate fate that now "everything [he does], goes down in doubt."[15]

That Shepard would employ a prologue and moreover have it serve its conventional function of stating "a moral point or anticipating the theme and action"[16] is, from a structural standpoint, particularly significant; not only does it reveal ipso facto that unlike *The Rock Garden*, *The Holy Ghostly*, and many of his other early works, *The Tooth of Crime* has a readily expressible theme, it also implies that the play will have a coherent course of dramatic action (culminating in the death of its hero). Furthermore, the fact that it is not a comparatively marginal character but the play's protagonist who delivers this prologue—and that it is as much a soliloquy as a thematic overview—serves both to establish Hoss as the play's *raisonneur*, against whose vision all others' are to be measured, and to further distinguish him from Shepard's earlier father figures.

Unlike Man in *The Rock Garden*, and Pop in *The Holy Ghostly*, who out of either fear or misplaced faith had buried themselves in the most narrow of existences, and therefore needed their sons to instruct them as to other ways of being and viewing the world, it is Hoss himself who has had an awareness, who is alert to (if not necessarily in harmony with) the ever-shifting strains of the Zeitgeist and who takes it upon himself to try to enlighten others.

In fact, it is Hoss's attempt to impart his vision to his handlers which makes up most of the first act's dramatic action. In one exchange after the next, Hoss seeks some corroboration for his uncertainty, for his vision of the world as a suddenly changed place, and for the ambivalence with which he views his own ascent. As he confides to Becky, his manager and one-time girlfriend:

> The game can't contain a true genius. It's too small. The next genius is gonna be a Gypsy Killer. I can feel it. I know it's goin' down right now. We don't have the whole picture. We're too successful. We're insulated from what's really happening by our own fame.[17]

Hoss has come to recognize the more debilitating and paradoxical aspects of his success. He has discovered that every victory is, in some way, an incapacitation, every reward a punishment, and that the higher he climbs, the closer he comes to his ultimate goal of going "gold,"[18] the more remote his original inspirations become, and the weaker and more precarious his resolve. Furthermore, Hoss has learned that achievement does not come without a psychospiritual price. Having initially thought that he could win on his own terms, that like his heroes—Dylan, Townshend, and Jagger[19]—he could both be his culture's idol and remain its adversary, Hoss now sees himself as an unwitting Faust, a naive figure who offered up his soul without somehow ever knowing it,[20] and who consequently is at risk of becoming the sort of man he has always despised:

> Can't you see what's happened to us? We ain't Markers no more. . . . We're punk chumps cowering under the Keepers and the Refs and the critics and the public eye. We ain't free no more! Goddamnit!. . . . We've become respectable and safe.[21]

For a self-purported iconoclast like Hoss to view himself as "respectable," as having forfeited his autonomy in exchange for group acceptance, is, perhaps, the ultimate denigration. Indeed, so intent is Hoss on eradicating this disgrace, and on returning to his disreputable roots, that he now appears willing to do the hitherto unthinkable: namely, give up his turf, turn his back on the Game, and begin again in a new direction.

It eventually becomes clear, however—as Hoss consults with one advisor after another—that as dissatisfied as he is with both himself and his situation, and as convinced as he is that he must do something, he has given no real thought as to what that 'thing' might be. Furthermore, the fact that Hoss feels compelled to argue his plans (such as they are) rather than simply act on them, is indicative of just how little autonomy he has left. Having habitually submitted to the will of his advisors, having allowed himself to be "molded and shaped . . . and sharpened down,"[22] Hoss—despite all his imperious posturing—has become, as Lynda Hart notes, "a puppet for those whom he believes to be his subordinates."[23] And although he does not overtly acknowledge himself as such, and in fact spends much of the first act considering whether to become a Gypsy, an anarchist, or a farmer "just livin' [his] life,"[24] it becomes increasingly apparent that unless he can gain his advisors' consent, Hoss will have no recourse but to remain on the road he is now on.[25]

As it turns out, no such consent is ever given. However genuine their concern for him, Hoss's advisors are neither altruists nor martyrs and are not about to sacrifice their own ambitions in order that Hoss may pursue his. Quite the contrary. Despite their outlandish garb and hip lingo, they are first and foremost business people who view Hoss as the means to their individual ends. For Becky, Starman, and Galactic Jack (and to a lesser extent, Doc and Cheyenne), Hoss is, as his name suggests, a means of transport, a vehicle who, if blindered and pointed in the right direction, if given the whip and carrot in equal measure, will ultimately carry them across the finish line and into a new world of wealth and privilege.

On their behalf, however, it can be argued that Hoss's advisors—whatever their self-interests—are only seeking that Hoss adhere to their original deal. They did fulfill their part, after all; they took a "complete beast of nature,"[26] and not only turned him into a well-honed fighting machine, a "killer's killer,"[27] but then dedicated the next twenty-odd years to his advancement. Now they expect Hoss to live up to his side of the bargain; he must either make it to the top of the charts or die trying. And for him to attempt to do otherwise, for Hoss—at this critical juncture—to question the significance of (and contemplate options to) the murderous career he had freely chosen, for him to suddenly concern himself with such irrelevant ephemera as "salvation" and the "original self" is—to his advisors' way of thinking—not only grossly impractical but morally insupportable. And indeed, when one considers that if Hoss were to suddenly depart his advisors would be left as empty handed as they were when they began some twenty years before, it becomes difficult to view their position as wholly unjustified.

So then who stands on the higher moral ground, Hoss or his advisors? The individual who in seeking personal salvation forsakes his responsibility to the group on whom he has long depended, or the group who in the name of fealty and collective prosperity inhibits and exploits the individual? Whose welfare finally, is of greater importance: one's own or that of the group to whom one is allied? It is a question to which Shepard has repeatedly returned throughout his career and to which he has responded differently at different times. In his early father-son plays, where the individual and group are represented respectively by the spiritually-minded son and materially-motivated father, Shepard's sympathies lie largely with the individual. However, in his later father-son plays—beginning with *Curse of the Starving Class*—when the individual in question is the father and the group he wishes to break free from is the family he has helped create and is obliged to love and support, Shepard's position becomes more ambiguous.

Accepting these distinctions, one may then classify *The Tooth of Crime* as not only belonging in part to each group but as being their transitional link. In fact, as one examines the play's two acts, the major conflicts therein, and the manner and degree in which their respective antagonists are morally differentiated, it becomes apparent that *The Tooth of Crime* divides neatly with its first act foreshadowing the later plays and its second act approximating the earlier ones. Much like their antecedents—Man and Boy, Ice and Pop—the antagonists in Act Two, Hoss and Crow, are in moral terms obviously antithetical. Theirs is a conflict, as Florence Falk points out, between the prototypical "good guy [and] . . . bad guy,"[28] whereas the conflict between Hoss and his advisors in Act One resembles those of Shepard's later family plays. Here the adversaries are closer to being moral equals and therefore the moral distinctions are of a more relative and subtle sort: the central question being not so much who is good and who is bad, nor for that matter who is right and who is wrong, but rather the thornier one of which set of self-interests is more ethically compelling.

In order to answer this question, we must first precisely define these self-interests. What exactly is it that Hoss and Becky each want? Let us focus first on Hoss. Perhaps the clearest articulation of his ambitions, of what he has lost and hopes to reclaim, is his lengthy monologue to Becky and Doc near the end of Act One. In it, Hoss tells the story of how, some twenty years earlier, he and his only two friends (the orphaned greaser, Cruise, and the big Creole kid, Moose) were set upon by a group of high school "rich . . . kids . . . hot for blood,"[29] and how, in the fight which ensued, he and his friends—despite their being outnumbered, unarmed, and the victims of what essentially was a suprise attack—were able to devastate their opponents:

> Then I saw it. This was a class war. . . . Soon as I saw that I flipped out. I found my strength. I started kickin' shit, man. . . . We had all eight of 'em bleeding and cryin' for Ma right there in the parking lot of Bob's Big Boy. I'll never forget that. The courage we had.[30]

This was, perhaps, Hoss's defining moment; the experience through which he discovered he was a true warrior, that he had a calling and was not another maladjusted, teen-age outcast. Morever, the fact that he "found . . . [his] strength" in the realization that this was "a class war," reveals that Hoss, at the very beginning of his career, was fueled first and foremost by moral outrage, by a clear and tangible connection to a moral universe of the sort he indirectly alludes to in his Prologue; one where inequalities and injustices are actively opposed, where the hero is looked upon with reverence, and where if the individual is "doin' time,"[31] it is only for his own crimes.[32]

It is this moral universe that Hoss now hopes to somehow rediscover. Feeling himself alone, unmoored, and responsible only to a weakening sense of self and a parasitic entourage, Hoss yearns to be once more in harmony with the moral world-at-large, to be waging war both for and *against* something bigger than himself. Having known material success in the extreme, having spent years living in a castle complete with moat, draw-bridge, armed checkpoints,[33] sex slaves[34] and a seemingly endless supply of drugs and liquors, Hoss now looks upon this way of life not as the happy fulfilment of his dreams, but as a fall from grace. He now sees success (insofar as it is defined by the Game) as an agent of immaturation, a force which infantilizes the individual by offering him unconditional access to a treasure trove of sensual pleasures, all the while cutting him off from the grittier, more nourishing realities which helped inspire and form him.[35]

On the other hand, for Becky and the rest, such "infantilization"— far from being thought a fall from grace—is a life long dream.[36] As Becky makes clear in her introductory song/soliloquy, "Nasty Times," what matters most is financial independence, the ability to live without Hoss in the same high style as she has with him. Impatient with "all these champeens and their killings . . . all these maggots—high heeled faggots,"[37] Becky is intent on Hoss making it to the top of the charts and on being duly rewarded when he does. For her, this is to be the ultimate score, the one which will allow her own state of grace. Finally, after decades of perseverance and of feeling, economically, like "a bucket full of holes,"[38] Becky will have the financial wherewithal to give full, free vent to her material appetites or, as she puts it, to "lay back in . . . [her] own."[39]

Having now looked at Hoss and Becky (and at what they each want), it remains, admittedly, still difficult to ascertain which of the two is the more morally compelling. Is the need to fight for a cause, for some abstract notion of "the good," in itself any more admirable, ethically speaking, than the need to escape economic servitude and stand financially on one's own two feet? And why, if Hoss's goals are of no greater moral value, does Shepard side with him so unequivocally? One reason may be that, as Florence Falk, Martin Tucker, and Charles Bachman point out, Hoss suffers; that he is far and away the play's most vulnerable and conflicted character.[40] But the deciding factor appears to be that Hoss's ambitions—in marked contrast to those of Becky and the rest—are essentially spiritual; and as earlier noted, in Shepard's hierarchy of values it is spiritual and not material wealth, the ineffable aspiration and not the corporeal one, which seems ultimately to matter.

It is to the degree that one shares these values that as Act One proceeds and Hoss is summarily dismissed by Becky and the rest as a "talkin loser"[41] with "buck fever"[42] and pushed back into a fray for which he is emotionally unprepared (and which he inevitably loses), that one experiences what Northrop Frye terms "a pitying sense of wrongness."[43] Indeed, to one so inclined, *The Tooth of Crime* is, in the Aristotelian sense, a rather "shocking"[44] play in that it presents the better man being defeated not only in the end, but at every turn along the way. Outargued and outmaneuvered by his advisors (most notably Becky)[45] in the first act, outbattled and utterly outdone by Crow in the second, Hoss's fortunes steadily and inexorably decline. So much so, in fact, that from a structural perspective, the play—in taking Hoss from doubt to estrangement, obsolescence, and finally, to death—seems to be essentially a two act, point-by-point corroboration of its Prologue.

*

In Crow, the Gypsy marker, we see a surrogate son whose unabashed dedication to power for its own sake distinguishes him not only from Hoss and the earlier sons but from every father and son in Shepard's canon. Utterly remorseless, impervious to doubt and so emotionally disengaged from his fellow man as to render all ideas of estrangement irrelevant, Crow is, as Shepard describes him,

> a totally lethal human being with no way or reason for tracing how he got that way. He just appeared. . . . He's simply following his more savage instincts. . . . He needed a victim, so I gave him one. He devoured him just like he was supposed to.[46]

Although Crow does not make his entrance until the very end of the first act, Shepard provides clues to his character much earlier on. Halfway through Act One, we learn that this utterly anonymous Gypsy, with neither colors nor turf, has somehow been able to "mark" (i.e., declare war on) Hoss, the Game's preeminent marker, and is, at present, crossing the border of "Zone five." Shortly thereafter, we observe Hoss command his men to "let . . . [Crow] through . . . all the way."[47]

Through these few bits of information, some sense of Crow's character begins to emerge. That he would dare declare war on the Game's preeminent marker suggests, in addition to courage and raw insolence, a contemptuous disregard for the Game's rules and protocols, and by extension the traditional American paths to success. Rather than patiently make his way up through the ranks, rather than subject himself (as Hoss did) to a period of honing and molding, Crow's apparent modus operandi is to immediately go for broke, either to rule the world right now or die in the attempt.

Furthermore, although Crow is willing to stake everything on this one fight, he is no military strategist. Quite the contrary; the fact that Crow needs to go through five "zones"[48] or checkpoints in order to then stand before an armed fortress in the mere hope of being granted entry suggests that his plan to unseat Hoss is, tactically speaking, little more than a suicide mission, and reveals Crow to be a fatalist who believes far more in good luck, blind courage, and the efficacy of the brash gesture than in well-conceived battle plans. Moreover, the fact that his tactics—as muddled as they are—*do succeed*, that Hoss does fortuitously intervene to "let him through"[49] (rather than have him killed or turned away), points to the possibility that Crow may be more than merely brazen; he may be destiny's child.

And so, while Shepard has yet to introduce Crow on-stage, he has nonetheless offered us enough expository information to form an impression of him as a brashly nihilistic, dangerously ambitious young warrior upon whom the gods smile—a man whose motives seem simple and pure (in a Darwinian sense), and of the sort which Nietzsche characterizes as:

> [the desire for strength to] manifest itself as strength, as the desire to overcome, to appropriate, to have enemies, obstacles, and triumphs.[50]

Having so hinted at Crow's character, Shepard proceeds then both to confirm and to expand upon these initial impressions at the very end of the first act. With his "huge shadow"[51] looming ominously "across the upstage wall behind Hoss,"[52] and his voice loudly echoing over "the P.A. system,"[53] the young Gypsy killer announces himself finally and unequivocally:

> Ever since I was good
> I wanted to be—evil
> Ever since I went bad
> I wanted to be—badder
>
> Ever since I was dead
> I wanted to be—born like a maniac
> And now that I got all that I wished
> I don't see me ever goin' back
>
> At the moment the angel grew in me
> I started to stangle her oh so tenderly
> I cried no you won't have me quite this easily
> I cried no, no, no you won't have me without a fight

Now that I kiss all that's deadly
What can touch me—even gently[54]

 While functioning obviously as a proclamation of character, Crow's soliloquy—most notably the first two and a half stanzas—may also be looked upon as the playwright's attempt to forge, however obliquely, his own definition of evil. In the opening lines of its first stanza ("Ever since I was good / I wanted to be evil") Shepard dispenses with the Christian concept of original sin by suggesting that unlike goodness—which he perceives as being inherent to Man—evil is something that one "wants to be"; it is an ambition towards which one must consciously strive. It is also, as stanza two makes clear, a state of being that if achieved precludes any possibility of redemption. Unlike the sinner who can conceivably atone for what he has done, the evil Self is immutable because, as the third stanza reveals, it has killed "the angel" within. It has permanently deformed itself in order to silence all internal opposition and allow certain drives and compulsions to exist unchecked. Moreover, the fact that in Shepard's cosmology "the angel" symbolizes not only the spiritual but the *female* aspect of self leads us to conclude that these unfettered drives are essentially male in character, and that for Shepard, it is the pure, masculine compulsion towards material self-satisfaction, devoid of all spiritual and humanistic concern, which constitutes evil.

*

 In a letter to Richard Schechner, Shepard describes *The Tooth of Crime* as being "like *High Noon*,"[55] and indeed the play and the film are similar in a number of significant ways. Both begin their plots rather late.[56] Both focus on a climactic showdown, the events leading immediately up to it, and its aftermath. Both feature reluctant, middle-aged protagonists who are estranged in some fundamental way from the communities in which they live, and yet—because they are men of a certain integrity and reputation—choose to risk their lives on behalf of these communities.
 Where the play and film do noticeably differ, structurally speaking, is in their respective resolutions. In *High Noon*, a work clearly intent on creating tension and suspense, the protagonist's fate remains uncertain right up until the moment it is happily decided. And while his victory is not completely unexpected,[57] what then ensues is somewhat

surprising.[58] In *The Tooth of Crime*, on the other hand, there is neither a triumphant surprise ending nor a comparable level of suspense. In fact, from a plot perspective, there are remarkably few surprises (although for the experienced viewer the lack of surprise, the lack of narrative misdirection, is admittedly something of a surprise in itself). Instead, what drives the plot forward is an ever more emphatic sense of inevitability.

From the very outset, from Hoss's soliloquy at the beginning of the first act, to his expressions of doubt and fatigue, through to his fateful decision to fight Crow on Crow's terms midway through the second act, almost everything said or done to or by him serves to foreshadow his defeat. In fact, one could describe *The Tooth of Crime* as a work where predestination subsumes free will, where the central dramatic question posed is neither "will the good man win?" (as it is in *High Noon*) nor "what need the good man now do to win?", but rather "what sort of world is this where the good man *cannot win*?"

Once Hoss acknowledges that he can neither escape the Game nor his own historical obsolescence, his behavior takes a self-destructive turn. Much like Joseph Campbell's archetypal hero who hears but does not heed the call, Hoss has lost "the power of significant positive action and [has] become a victim to be saved."[59] Rather than "retreat from the world scene"[60] and journey beyond the Game "inward into depths where obscure resistances are overcome, and long lost powers are revivified,"[61] Hoss has chosen to stay his present course and, as a consequence, is not only unable to forestall "the gradual approach of his disintegration"[62] but appears now to be actively soliciting it. First he demands that Crow, a man intent on killing him, be allowed to enter his castle unhindered, and then, after sizing him up, inexplicably plays to the young Gypsy's strengths by agreeing to a "style match"— a form of combat with which he is altogether unfamiliar.

He does this (or so he maintains) in order to revitalize himself, to be once more the underdog and re-experience real risk. It is clear however, that there exist far darker reasons for this decision—reasons which he expresses only indirectly. At the end of the first act, an angry, dispirited Hoss confesses to Becky that he is "ready to take it all on. The whole shot. The big one."[63] And although these lines can obviously be interpreted in a number of ways, when one considers how often Hoss alludes to an overwhelming world-weariness, a happy past long gone, and to having, in general, irretrievably lost his way, one cannot help but ascribe to them a certain ominous significance.

Hoss, it appears, is intent not on rejuvenation but, as Robert Coe points out, on his own annihilation,[64] and with this end in mind, has quite capriciously decided upon this particular Gypsy mark as the Oedipus to his Laius.

But in order that he be defeated by a man such as Crow, Hoss must first stack the deck against himself. Hence, he refuses to do battle in the ways he is expert (i.e., those which utilize any "kinda' weapon or machine")[65] committing his fate instead to a war of words. The "style match" to which we had earlier alluded is, in fact, a song duel, an extemporaneous exchange of verbal thrusts and parries, where the objective is to "stab" one's opponent with a truth that is so cruel and unopposable that it psychologically immobilizes him.

In such a contest, to have a clearly articulated sense of self, to attach oneself to belief systems and behavioral codes—in essence, to subscribe to anything outside of one's own primal appetites—is to render oneself readily accessible to attack. Hence, it is Hoss, the father surrogate, who proves to be the easier target. Frequently outraged by what he considers to be Crow's misrepresentations, as well as by his methods, Hoss fritters away his energy and focus by arguing first with the Gypsy and then the referee over what one tactically can and cannot do. Crow, on the other hand, is able to "lie flat on his back and relax completely"[66] between rounds. Possessing neither a readily definable sense of self nor an extensive set of values, Crow can far more casually slip and dodge Hoss's verbal blows (the number of his exclamatory reactions are in fact half those of Hoss). This allows him to concentrate on his offensive attacks, and eventually Crow puts together such a furious flurry of insults and castigations that the referee stops the fight, awarding the young Gypsy "son" an Oedipal victory by technical knockout.

This decision, in turn, puts Hoss over the edge. Incensed by what he considers a ridiculously unjust decision, he shoots and kills the referee, thereby placing himself outside the Game once and for all. Now Hoss must learn another way of being. Having lost his turf, having suddenly become, in essence, a Gypsy, he must now learn from Crow how to think and act like one:

> No . . . lookin in. Back at yerself. You gotta look out. Straight into me and out the back a' my head. . . . Cut me in half. Get mean. There's too much pity, man. Too much empathy . . . Use yer eyes like a weapon. . . Always on the offence.[67]

Try as he may however, Hoss is unable to reinvent himself. Much like Man and Pop before him, he cannot reconcile himself to the new world which his "son" personifies. Ultimately incapable of renouncing the values, beliefs, and behavior that had long served as a source of strength, and that had, in fact, helped make him the Game's preeminent marker, Hoss is driven in the end to sacrifice his life to them. With Crow coolly looking on, Hoss shoots himself, thereby fulfilling a destiny for which we, the audience, have long been prepared.

Immediately thereafter, Becky reappears on stage, not to mourn Hoss but to ally herself with the new champion.[68] Driven by self-interests of the most narrow sort, she is, in fact, utterly untouched by the death of her one-time boyfriend and long-time collaborator.

> CROW   Becky, get some biceps to drag out these stiffs. Get the place lookin' a little decent. We're gonna have us a celebration.
>
> BECKY   I had a feeling you'd take him. Was it hard?
>
> CROW   Yeah. He was pretty tough. Went out in the old style. Clung right up to the end.
>
> BECKY   He was a good Marker man. One a' the great ones.
>
> CROW   Not great enough.
>
> BECKY   I guess not.[69]

Here again, at the play's end, Shepard makes the point that in a brave new nihilistic world such as this, where a new generation of half-men rule and where the size of one's trough is all that matters, the old idea (as personfied by Hoss, the "father") of dying to preserve one's integrity, of sacrificing oneself to anything as nebulous as an ideal, is looked upon as something ridiculous and unfathomable.

Notes

1. Both Bonnie Marranca and Ron Mottram emphasize the significance of the play's language. Marranca declares that "*Tooth* is about making up language and using it to manipulate reality." Mottram goes even further, stating that "In *Tooth of Crime*, more than any of his other plays, Shepard gave the theatre back to language. Setting, action, plot, are all sacrificed to the power of the word." One may argue, however, that by having Hoss and Crow resolve their fates via a climactic "style match," a war of words, Shepard, rather than subordinating plot to language, is able to successfully integrate the two. See Bonnie Mannanca "Alphabetical Shepard: A Play of Words," *American Dreams: The Imagination of Sam Shepard*, ed. Bonnie Marranca (New York: Performing Arts Journal Publications, 1981), 25, and Ron Mottram, *Inner Landscapes* (Columbia: University of Missouri Press, 1984), 108.

2. Richard Gilman considers *The Tooth of Crime* Shepard's finest play, stating that it is "the one play which is most nearly invulnerable to charges of occlusion, or arbitrary procedure, the one that rests most self-containedly, that seems whole, inevitable, settled." Introduction to *Sam Shepard: Seven Plays* (New York: Bantam Books, 1981), xxi.

3. Stanley Kauffmann similarly praises *The Tooth of Crime* "as the best work of his I know" and for similar reasons: "[It] completes what it starts in the form in which it is put." See "What Price Freedom?" *American Dreams*, 106.

4. Vivian Paraka and Mark Siegel view *The Tooth of Crime* as "designed to persuade us that what is coming is worse." *Sam Shepard* (Boise, ID: Boise State University Press, 1985), 26.

5. Robert Coe points out that "while Shepard identifies deeply with both Crow and Hoss . . . his deeper and more crucial allegiances are with Hoss." See Robert Coe, "Image Shots Are Blown: The Rock Plays," *American Dreams*, 65.

6. Sam Shepard, *The Tooth of Crime* in *The Tooth of Crime and The Geography of A Horse Dreamer* (New York: Grove Press, 1974), 22.

7. Ibid., 3.

8. Ibid.

9. However, what most dramatically distinguishes Hoss from Shepard's earlier father figures (as well as his later ones) is neither his high status nor his expertise in all manners of violence but rather that he is a warrior-*artist* whose intuitive powers and propensity for doubt and self-examination show him to be as much a descendent of Christopher Marlowe and Francois Villon as he is of Elvis and Wyatt Earp.

10 Herbert Marcuse, "Varieties of Humanism," *Center Magazine*, June 1968, 14.

11 *The Tooth of Crime*, 4.

12 Ibid.

13 Ibid.

14 Ibid.

15 Ibid.

16 Karl Beckson and Arthur Ganz, *A Reader's Guide to Literary Terms: A Dictionary* (New York: Farrar, Strauss and Giroux, 1960), 165.

17 *The Tooth of Crime*, 11.

18 Ibid., 22.

19 Ibid., 10.

20 Hoss's present circumstance, while exacerbated by his advisors' insentivity, is nonetheless an outgrowth of his own ambitions. His handlers, in fact, are the mere embodiment of that ambition, the collective Mephistopheles to whom, in exchange for power, glory, and riches, he offered himself.

21 *The Tooth of Crime*, 22.

22 Ibid., 11.

23 *Sam Shepard's Metaphorical Stages* (New York: Greenwood Press, 1987), 52.

24 *The Tooth of Crime*, 16.

25 Hoss now finds himself in the terribly ironic position of needing permission to be free. He is like an incarcerated king whose only means to freedom is petition, and whose wardens, if they defer to him at all, do so out of a certain sense of decorum and because they realize that a marginally unhappy prisoner is better than a woefully miserable one.

26 *The Tooth of Crime*, 11.

27 Ibid.

28 "Men Without Women: The Shepard Landscape," *American Dreams*, 93.

29 *The Tooth of Crime*, 35.

30 Ibid.

31 Ibid., 4.

32 Surprisingly, none of the critics consulted see this monologue, in which Hoss clearly articulates the moral values he had lost and somehow hopes to regain,

as exceptionally significant. Only Florence Falk accords it any importance, stating that "Hoss's fondest memories are of the days when he, Moose, and Cruise 'ran together'." "Men Without Women: The Shepard Landscape," *American Dreams*, 97.

33 *The Tooth of Crime*, 31.

34 Ibid., 42.

35 Unlike, say, a prizefighter who needs to be isolated in order to best prepare for his next fight, Hoss being a warrior-artist feels that the isolation afforded him by his success has in fact weakened him.

36 To Becky et al., who have willingly given up their scruples in return for status and security, the Faustian exchange of one's soul for earthly power is an exceedingly good deal, a near steal in fact—as close to getting something for nothing as they can possibly imagine.

37 *The Tooth of Crime*, 9.

38 Ibid.

39 Ibid.

40 Florence Falk describes Hoss as "having too much heart," while Martin Tucker characterizes him as an "innately decent [man who] . . . comes from an earlier tradition that allows for such humanistic options as emotion and projective sympathy." See Florence Falk, "Men Without Women: The Shepard Landscape," 94, and Martin Tucker, *Sam Shepard* (New York: Continuum, 1992) 89. Similarly, Charles Bachman sees Hoss essentially as a figure "troubled by his humanity . . . [by his capacity for] pity . . . [and] empathy." See "Defusion of Menace in the Plays of Sam Shepard," *Essays on American Drama: Williams, Miller, Albee, and Shepard*, ed., Dorothy Parker (Toronto: University of Toronto Press, 1987), 168.

41 *The Tooth of Crime*, 11.

42 Ibid.

43 In his analysis of tragedy, Northrop Frye describes the genre as "a paradoxical combination of a fearful sense of rightness (the hero must fall) and a pitying sense of wrongness (it is too bad that he falls)." *The Anatomy of Criticism* (Princeton, NJ: Princeton University Press, 1957), 214. Accepting such a definition, one might then argue that Hoss certainly has some of the attributes of a tragic hero.

44 In Chapter Thirteen of the *Poetics*, Aristotle declares "the spectacle of a virtuous man being brought from prosperity to adversity" to be incapable of arousing pity and fear, rather "it merely shocks us." *Poetics*, trans. S.H. Butcher (New York: Hill and Wang, 1961), 75.

45 When one takes into account that in Act One it is Becky who most effectively rebuts Hoss's plan to forsake the Game, and who, in fact, decides that Hoss

should fight Crow with "shivs" (knives) even though Hoss protests that he "ain't used a blade for over ten years," it becomes difficult to wholly accept Florence Falk's characterization of Becky as someone who merely "snaps to attention whenever Hoss calls." See "Men Without Women: The Shepard Landscape," 96.

46 Sam Shepard, "Language, Visualization, and the Inner Library," *American Dreams*, 217.

47 *The Tooth of Crime*, 31.

48 Ibid.

49 Ibid.

50 Friedrich Nietzsche, *The Birth of Tragedy and The Genealogy of Morals*, trans. Francis Golffing (Garden City, NY: Doubleday, 1956), 178.

51 *The Tooth of Crime*, 39.

52 Ibid.

53 Ibid.

54 Ibid., 39–40.

55 Quoted in Richard Schechner, "The Writer and The Performance Group: Rehearsing *The Tooth of Crime*," *American Dreams*, 166.

56 Ruby Cohn, *New American Dramatists 1960–1980* (New York: Grove Press, 1982), 181.

57 The fact that *High Noon* is a Hollywood western which stars Gary Cooper as its sheriff-protagonist creates, in and of itself, certain expectations as to its resolution.

58 Having demonstrated his competence and courage, Cooper tosses away his sheriff's badge and then rides off, leaving the community to fend for itself.

59 Joseph Campbell, *The Hero With A Thousand Faces* (Princeton, NJ: Princeton University Press, 1949), 59.

60 Ibid., 17.

61 Ibid., 29.

62 Ibid., 59.

63 *The Tooth of Crime*, 37.

64 Coe states that "being suicidal is part of Hoss's nature." See "Image Shots Are Blown," 63.

65 *The Tooth of Crime*, 52.

66 Ibid., 55.

67 Ibid., 66.

68 In transferring her allegiance to Crow, Becky has rendered his Oedipal triumph complete; for not only has the Gypsy "son" destroyed the "father," he has won the "mother" as well.

69 *The Tooth of Crime*, 74.

Chapter Four

Curse of the Starving Class: Biology (Alas) Is Destiny

With *Curse of the Starving Class*, written in 1976, Shepard embarks upon a series of plays in which the father-son conflict appears not as a singular phenomenon without any ramifications beyond itself, but in the context of family life as a whole. For the first time, we see the relationships between husband and wife, mother and son, and father and daughter accorded the same dramatic significance as that between father and son.

What further distinguishes *Curse of the Starving Class* from Shepard's earlier father-son plays is that here the father, Weston Tate, and his son, Wesley, while clearly antagonistic towards one another at times, are not, in any real sense, adversaries. Unlike the mythic fathers and sons of *The Holy Ghostly* and *The Tooth of Crime*, who as representatives of warring cosmologies do battle to the death in semiabstract seclusion, Weston and Wesley are (in their own confused and idiosyncratic way) allies, linked to one another by blood, environment, and mutual concern. Furthermore, one could argue that it is Ella, Weston's wife and Wesley's mother, who is the play's antagonist, and that Weston's relationship to his son is more analogous to that of the Ghost and Hamlet than that of Laius to Oedipus.

This bond between father and son is revealed at the play's outset. *Curse* begins with Wesley matter-of-factly shoveling up the remains of a front door Weston had drunkenly smashed a few hours earlier.[1] Unlike Ice and Crow who preyed upon their fathers' weaknesses, Wesley both accepts his father's failings and takes it upon himself to somehow compensate for them. Here is a character hitherto unseen in Shepard's work: the son as martyr, who aspires to make right his father's wrongs in the hope of somehow saving him. Wesley's loyalties are, in fact, so fierce and so singular that even when Weston is clearly in the wrong (as he was earlier that day), Wesley will not blame him:

WESLEY [Weston] wasn't threatening you.
ELLA   Are you kidding me? He broke the door down didn't he?
WESLEY He was just trying to get in.
ELLA   That's no way to get into a house. . . .
WESLEY He was drunk.
ELLA   That's not my problem.
       . . . .
WESLEY How come you called the cops?
ELLA   I was scared.
WESLEY You thought he was going to kill you?
ELLA   I thought—I thought, "I don't know who this is. . . ."
WESLEY I heard you screaming at each other.
ELLA   Yes.
WESLEY So you must've known who it was.
       . . . .
WESLEY It's humiliating to have the cops come to your own house. Makes me feel like we're someone else . . . like we're in trouble or something.
ELLA   We're not in trouble. He's in trouble. . . .[2]

As this exchange makes clear, it is not his father's actions but their public disclosure which most troubles Wesley. It is also apparent that while he looks upon Weston as a helpless innocent, as a drunkard, who though often destructive and contentious, is no more morally accountable for his actions than a bear in the woods, he is decidedly less charitable towards his mother. As far as Wesley is concerned, it is Ella who in seeking help outside the family becomes the true transgressor. In fact, by calling in the authorities, his mother has committed *two* unpardonable sins: not only has she made the Tates' problems a matter of public record, but she has moreover declared these problems to be so extreme that now if the family is to survive at all, it must forfeit its autonomy.

At first, Wesley resists his mother's definition of things, accusing her, in effect, of lying, of grossly exaggerating her danger in order to exact some petty revenge. But try as he may to dismiss Ella's call to the police as utterly unwarranted, as a vindictive indulgence directed towards his father, Wesley must concede in the end that his family really "is in trouble,"[3]—vulnerable, according to Doris Auerbach, to both "destructive forces . . . [which attempt to] crush it from without and . . . disintegration from within."[4] Indeed, by threatening Weston with arrest and imprisonment, Ella has, in Wesley's eyes, more than sullied the family's reputation (such as it is); she has made it painfully clear that even familial love is conditional, and that there may come a moment, when for the sake of the its members, the family need be destroyed.

Ella herself admits as much when she declares that it is not the family in general (i.e., Wesley, her twelve year old daughter, Emma, and herself) but Weston alone who "is in trouble."[5] Having watched her marriage deteriorate over the years as the result of her husband's drunkenness, his financial irresponsibility, and general neglect, Ella, unlike her son, has come to accept the inviolable family to be but an ideal towards which one strives, and not an incontrovertible fact of nature. Furthermore, she realizes that in the face of her family's imminent unraveling all she can do is try to save those who can be saved, and it is towards that end that she now plans, with the help of Taylor, an ersatz lawyer, to sell the farm without Weston's knowledge, and with the money move herself and her children to Europe.

Unsurprisingly, Ella's plan meets with immediate resistance. Wesley, who still hopes to "join [with Weston] that . . . avocado association"[6] and "work this place by ourselves,"[7] sees this emigration as both treasonous and absurd. Why, he jingoistically argues, should he go all the way to Europe to see "high Art . . . castles and fancy food"[8] when "they got all that stuff here."[9] Emma also opposes her mother's scheme, and, generally speaking, on similar grounds. Like her brother, she regards Ella's plan as divisive and fundamentally pointless, albeit admittedly for different reasons:

> EMMA You mean just you, me, and Wes are going to Europe? That sounds awful.
> ELLA Why? What's so awful about that? It could be a vacation.
> EMMA It'd be the same as here.
> ELLA No, it wouldn't! We'd be in Europe. A whole new place.
> EMMA But we'd all be the same people.
> ELLA What's the matter with you? Why do you say things like that?
> EMMA Well, we would be.[10]

As far as Emma is concerned, a move to Europe would have little effect on the Tates. They'd still "be the same people"[11] no matter where they fled to. Implicit in Emma's opposition is the belief that it is heredity, or more precisely, the socio-biological environment of the family in contrast to the socio-physical environment of the world at large, which determines one's identity and fate. And, in fact, the idea that "biology [alas] is destiny" is set forth so often throughout *Curse of the Starving Class*, and by so many of its characters, that one ultimately must regard it as the play's central theme.

Besides its thematic significance, Emma's response is also part of an interactional pattern to which the entire family eventually falls prey. By flatly dismissing the plan her mother has long nurtured, Emma adheres to what appears to be an unspoken dictum among the Tates: namely, that no hope be allowed to flourish no matter how briefly. Moreover, when one considers the unfailing, almost Pavlovian consistency with which each family member disparages the hopes and aspirations of the others, one recognizes that this is one aspect of the Tate family "curse."

An earlier and more dramatic example of the "curse" at work occurs when Emma, in an attempt to accord her life some degree of normalcy and order, appears onstage dressed in her 4-H Club uniform and carrying her 4-H Club charts. Immediately, she meets with resistance. First her mother confesses to having thoughtlessly cooked and eaten Emma's prized chicken. Then her brother, in an attempt to make it absolutely clear just how aberrant and unsafe this family is, urinates on her charts. Subsequently chastised by his mother for only "making things worse,"[12] Wesley counters by stating that, all appearances to the contrary, his cruelty is, in fact, a kindness.

> I'm opening up new possibilities for her. Now she'll have to do something else. It could change her whole direction in life. She'll look back and remember the day her brother pissed all over her charts [just as he himself will recall the night his mother called in the police] and see that day as a turning point in her life.[13]

The essential message that each Tate seems intent on communicating to the others is that they are each alone; that the family is but an ephemeral construct destined to collapse; and that consequently, they would each be wise to come up with some sort of plan to insure their individual survival.

And as it turns out, each family member does come up with an alternative course of action which, generally speaking, demands that he or she dissociate from the family (or at least part of it) in the hope of finally prospering. Hence, while Ella is intent on moving to Europe, Emma is bound for Mexico (to become a car mechanic), and Wesley to

Alaska. Even Weston has comes up with a new plan. In a dramatic turnabout, the family's fugitive-in-residence, the one family member who does in fact leave, and leave often, has decided suddenly, in one of his few sober moments, to stay put, rebuild the farm, and "happily" reunite the family.

As disparate as these plans may be, what they do have in common is their insubstantiality. They are rather more like daydreams than practical courses of action, and it is significant to note that neither the parents' nor the children's plans are successfully realized, albeit for different reasons.

The parents' failures are due largely to circumstances of their own making. Ella cannot sell the farm and move to Europe because as it turns out, Weston, while in a blackout, has already sold it to the bar owner, Ellis. Similarly, Weston cannot resurrect the farm because it is no longer his to resurrect. Nor, for that matter, can he reunify his family. It is, in fact, one of the play's more obvious ironies that no sooner does Weston realize that the happiness he "kept looking for . . . out there somewhere"[14] was "all the time . . . right inside this house,"[15] than he is again forced to abandon his family and flee to Mexico.

The children, on the other hand, fail to escape in part because they are deeply ambivalent about leaving and would prefer that their parents reconcile, and in part because of their intense loyalty to Weston. Inextricably bound to their father for reasons we shall explore shortly, both children repeatedly do battle with the world in Weston's defense. They not only, as already noted, contest Ella's plans and berate and insult Taylor, her co-conspirator and possible boyfriend, but eventually, as Weston's problems escalate, try to rectify matters by physical force. First, Emma destroys Ellis's bar in revenge for his having swindled her father out of the farm (for a mere fifteen hundred dollars). Then, when Ellis takes back the fifteen hundred dollars, citing the damage done by Emma, Wesley goes forth to reclaim it—only to return beaten-up and empty-handed.

As these heroics make clear, the roles of parent and child within the Tate family have become unfixed and interchangeable. In the face of Ella's and Weston's egocentrism, their inability to subordinate their own particular desires to those of the family as a whole, it is Wesley and Emma who—despite their youth and inexperience—try to serve as the family's protectors and caretakers. Here, as in *The Holy Ghostly* and *The Tooth of Crime*, we see the parent and child exchange identities. But what distinguishes *Curse of the Starving Class* from those earlier father-son plays is that in this work the father is not coerced by his son or daughter to relinquish his crown. Here, as in *The Rock Garden*, there are no great Oedipal showdowns, no shoot-outs or song duels; instead what we see is a father who had surrendered his claim to leadership long before the drama begins and the frantic, ineffectual attempts by his wife and children to fill the void left by him.

Yet, despite his abnegation, it is to Weston and not to Ella that the younger Tates pledge their allegiance. What is it precisely that motivates them? Why do Wesley and Emma go so far as to literally risk their lives for a man who has so consistently disappointed and abandoned them, and, conversely, show so little appreciation for their mother? Hasn't it been Ella, though she confesses to having done but "the bare minimum,"[16] who has nonetheless proven the more dutiful and caring parent? Isn't it she who keeps the family fed, who comes home with bags of groceries (in contrast to Weston who returns with but an armful of half-priced artichokes)? Certainly, her conception of the future seems to be the less selfish, and the more inclusive of the two: her plan, after all, is to sell the farm in order to go to Europe *with* her children. Weston's, on the other hand, is to unload his land, pay off his drinking debts, and disappear—leaving his suddenly destitute family to fend for itself.

An explanation for this disturbing though not unusual paradox may be found in a dialogue between Ella and Weston late in the play:

> WESTON   Well, she [Emma] always was a fireball.
> ELLA   Part of the inheritance, right?
> WESTON   Right. Direct inheritance.
> ELLA   Well, I'm glad you've found a way of turning shame into a source of pride.
> WESTON   What's shameful about it? Takes courage to get charged with all that stuff. It's not everyone her age who can run up a list of credits like that.
> ELLA   That's for sure.
> WESTON   Could you?
> ELLA   Don't be ridiculous! I'm not self-destructive. Doesn't run in the family line.
> WESTON   That's right. I never thought about it like that. You're the only one who doesn't have it. Only us.
> ELLA   Oh, so now I'm the outsider.
> WESTON   Well it's true. You come from a different class of people. Gentle. . . .[17]

As this exchange makes clear, intrafamily loyalty is determined not by action but by genealogy, by what one has biologically inherited from whom. It seems to be Shepard's contention that opposites do not attract (at least in regard to parents and children), that the more a child temperamentally and behaviorally resembles a particular parent, the more unshakable the bond between them. Consequently, despite Weston's chronic absenteeism and general indifference, he remains at the psychological and emotional center of his children's lives since it is he whom they most resemble. The passion, courage, and readiness for action that Wesley and Emma demonstrate have been inherited from him.

There is, however, as Ella points out, a dark side to this inheritance, namely that among the Tates passion and courage tend to manifest themselves self-destructively. And it is upon this dark side that the play primarily focusses. The curse that Shepard refers to in the play's title is not, as one might initially expect, a socio-economic curse, but a hereditary one which Benedict Nightingale accurately describes as the "inexorable handing over of loss from one generation to the next,"[18] and which Ella herself laments as being:

> always there. It comes onto us like a nightmare. Every day I can feel it. Every day I can see it coming. And it always comes. Repeats itself. It comes even when you do everything to stop it from coming. Even when you try to change it. And it goes back. Deep. It goes back and back to tiny little cells and genes. To atoms. To tiny little swimming things making up their minds without us. Plotting in the wombs.[19]

Heredity, in *Curse of The Starving Class*, functions in much the same way as the spiritual world does in *The Holy Ghostly*, and the emerging Zeitgeist, as personified by Crow, does in *The Tooth of Crime*—that is, as a great, inexorable force which the protagonist cannot fully acknowledge until it has destroyed him.[20]

Among the Tates, it is Wesley who most strenuously resists heredity's claim and whose eventual capitulation is consequently the most dramatic. Early in the play Wesley admits to certain nebulous fears which are somehow connected with his father:

> I could feel the space around like a big, black world. I listened like an animal. My listening was afraid. Afraid of sound. Tense. Like any second something could invade me. Some foreigner. Then I heard the Packard coming up the hill. . . .Then I could picture my Dad driving it.[21]

Here is the first, admittedly oblique, reference to a hereditary curse. What Wesley is afraid of is some yet unnamed, invasive force which will attack his identity rather than destroy him outright, and which he associates, however subconsciously, with Weston.

At the beginning of the second act, Wesley seems to disavow his earlier fears. Now, as far as he is concerned, the family's difficulties are simply the result of economic bad luck, of being always pressured to come up with temporary solutions to an ever-snowballing set of financial problems.

> WESLEY   She [Ella] can't think. He [Weston] can't either.
> EMMA   Don't be too harsh.
> WESLEY   How can they think when they're behind the eight ball all the time. They don't have time to think.[22]

By perceiving his parents' difficulties as external to them, as circumstantial rather than biologically predestined, Wesley can regard them as remediable. Such thinking still allows him to believe in the possiblity of right action and free will. It explains why, in the face of the family's imminent dissolution, he continues to do repairs and care for the livestock (most notably a sick lamb). In attempting to maintain the farm,[23] Wesley hopes first to remind his parents that there are things which can still be done to keep the family together and financially afloat, and second, to prove to himself that there is no hereditary curse, that rather than being the wastrel son of a wastrel father, he is an autonomous and disciplined individual who in many ways is the opposite of Weston.

It is not until late in the second act, during a pivotal exchange with Weston, that Wesley finally acknowledges the existence of a family curse. He does not, however, admit to having it. Nor, for that matter, does his father. In fact, not only does Weston contend that Wesley has escaped the curse (unlike himself and *his* father) but he also insinuates that he is responsible for his son being spared.

> WESTON   . . . Look at my outlook. You don't envy it right?
> WESLEY   No.
> WESTON   That's because it's full of poison. Infected. And you recognize poison, right? You recognize it when you see it?
> WESLEY   Yes.
>
> . . . .
>
> WESTON   Good. You're growing up. I never saw my old man's poison until I was much older than you. Much older. And then you know how I recognized it?

WESLEY How?
WESTON Because I saw myself infected with it. That's how. I saw me carrying it around. His poison in my body. You think that's fair?[24]

The point of this exchange, as far as Weston is concerned, is to put his son on alert. Repeatedly, he demands that Wesley perceive him as "poisoned," contending that the key to breaking free of one's genetic legacy is to be forewarned. Weston's great misfortune, or so he claims, was that he never knew of the curse's existence until it had already infected him. Implicit in this claim is the belief that the curse (and therefore, heredity itself) is circumventible through right action,[25] and that had he been alerted in advance, Weston too would have been able to somehow surmount its effects.

It is this belief, as naive and hubristic as it proves to be, which allows us to regard Weston's behavior towards his children in a slightly more favorable light. Weston, it appears, is not merely an irresponsible drunk after all. Rather, he is a complex and paradoxical figure who abandons his wife and kids in order to both escape their overwhelming demands *and* save them from his "poison." Not only is Weston, as Charles R. Lyons points out, "the problematic father"[26] from whom his children need be protected; he is also, paradoxically, their would-be protector who by unequivocally announcing himself as "infected" seeks to alert Wesley and Emma (as he himself was not alerted) and hopefully divert them from his path.

Weston not only declares himself "poisoned," he reveals it through his actions as well. We can, in fact, look at his drunkenness, belligerence, and general fecklessness, and see in their very flagrance an incontrovertible warning. For all his shortcomings, Weston does not attempt to disguise or misrepresent himself. He is neither a closet drinker nor a charmer engendering false hopes, but rather a conspicuous drunkard and truth-sayer who is not above telling his twelve-year-old daughter that "there's no protection"[27] and that she had "better think of something fast [to do with her life]"[28] because he has sold the farm in order to pay his debts.

Consequently, one may contend that Weston's indifference towards, and abuse of, his children is motivated, at least in part, by love. Furthermore, it is this love, as perverse and riddled with self-contempt as it admittedly is, which distinguishes Weston's relationship with Wesley (and Emma) from the relationships we analyzed in the previous plays. Here is a father and son who do sincerely care about one another, and who, instead of trying to destroy each other, are in their sad, limited ways doing whatever they can to try to insure each other's survival.

Ultimately, however, Weston and his son cannot protect one another and it is in the last act that we see both Wesley finally fall prey to the family curse and Weston disappear to Mexico. Ironically, Shepard begins the act on a note of high optimism. For the first time in the play, we see Weston sober. He has bathed, dressed in clean clothes, done the family laundry, and is now preparing a big breakfast. More significantly, Weston has had a complete change of heart regarding both his family and the farm. He tells Wesley:

> a family wasn't just a social thing. It was an animal thing. It was a reason of nature that we were all together under the same roof. Not that we had to be but we were supposed to be. And I started feeling glad about it. I started to feel full of hope.[29]

Demonstrating what Bonnie Marranca terms "the characteristic American [belief in] . . . rebirth, and its opposite, the denial of history,"[30] Weston, now spiritually and physically revivified, has decided to stay. He plans to rebuild the farm and, following Wesley's advice, to join the Avocado Growers Association.[31] It is at this very moment that the curse strikes. No sooner does the father proffer a hopeful course of action than the son reappears to strike it down. Having re-emerged halfway through the third act dressed in Weston's discarded shoes, cap, and coat, Wesley has finally become that which he has long struggled against. He is not, as Bonnie Marranca claims, the sole family member to escape "emotional devastation."[32] Quite the contrary. Wesley is now his father's Doppelganger, his delirious and suddenly insatiable double. In fact, Wesley has become so mad with "the curse" that he—in an act rife with symbolic significance—slaughters the lamb which earlier he had been trying to save.

> WESTON I can't fathom you, that's for sure. What'd you do with that lamb?
> WESLEY Butchered it.
> WESTON (turning away from him, disgusted) I swear to God. (pause, then turning to WESLEY) WHAT'D YA' BUTCHER THE DUMB THING FOR!
> WESLEY We need food.
> WESTON THE ICE BOX IS CRAMMED FULL A' FOOD!. . . . WHAT'D YA GO AND BUTCHER IT FOR? HE WAS GETTING BETTER![33]

Shepard uses the lamb as a free floating symbol to which he ascribes different meanings at different times. While functioning generally throughout the play as a symbol of hope, frailty, and goodness, the lamb serves more specifically (during Acts One and Two) as a symbol for the Tates. Like the family, the lamb suffers from an incapacitating disease which attacks it from the inside out and against which, alone, it is helpless. Furthermore, both the lamb and the Tates depend, in varying degrees, on Wesley for protection. He is their would-be savior, the family member who, be it by relocating their homes or going forth to battle their enemies, most actively attempts to insure their survival.

At the beginning of the third act, the lamb acquires yet another symbolic meaning. While continuing to serve as both a manifestation of Wesley's love and an evocation of the family, the lamb is also now linked symbolically to Weston. Ever the egocentric despite his rebirth, Weston sees the animal as representative of himself, as something which like him has a never-ending capacity for renewal, for "getting better."[34]

Hence, when the lamb is slaughtered by Weston's curse-ridden son, that which it symbolizes is also destroyed. It is this sacrifice which demonstrates, once and for all, heredity's utter omnipotence. Despite the family's attempts at circumvention, despite their recognitions and forewarnings, the "curse" has proven inescapable. We now see the Tates as having existed all along in a hopelessly deterministic universe where action is without effect, where love has lost its power to transform, and where a family's fate is irrevocably decided at the moment of its inception.

In the face of Wesley's transmutation and heredity's incontrovertible power, Weston stubbornly persists, albeit ever more unconvincingly, in seeing himself the cause of his family's misfortunes. As he watches his "starving"[35] derelict son stuff himself with scraps of food both from the ice box and off the floor, Weston launches into an explanation as to how and why he failed as a father.

> I couldn't stand it here. I couldn't stand the idea that everything would be the same. That every morning it would be the same. I kept looking for it out there somewhere. I kept trying to piece it together. The jumps. I couldn't figure out the jumps. From being born, to growing up, to droppin' bombs, to having kids, to hittin' bars, to this. It all turned around on me somehow. . . . I kept looking for it somewhere. And all the time it was right inside this house.[36]

In this confession fraught with contradictions, Weston sees himself alternately as a victim, a man abruptly and inexplicably dropped down into situations over which he had no control, and conversely as someone presented with clear opportunities for happiness ("right inside this house") but who failed consistently to recognize them. Weston's great character flaw, as he himself defines it, was that he never considered working the land or raising a family rich enough experiences in and of themselves. A man long accustomed to cataclysms (to sudden, dramatic transportations), he mistook a life of small, daily, almost imperceptible changes for one of utter stagnation, and so instead led a life of desperate improvisation where each failed experiment served only to drive him further from what he sought.

Later in the same act, Ella has a similar recognition. She too realizes finally what she should do but, like her husband's, her realization comes too late. It is one of the play's crueler ironies that the moment Ella puts her foot down, the moment she declares herself unequivocally "responsible"[37] for her daughter's welfare, is the very instant when Emma, in an attempt to flee her family once and for all, dies in a car-bomb explosion set by Weston's creditors.

The fact that both parents eventually claim responsibility for their derelictions, and in so doing claim some modicum of free will, in a play whose central theme is man's utter powerlessness in the face of heredity's intractable stamp, reveals in Shepard a deep ambivalence. Try as he may either to exonerate or blame Weston and Ella, he can ultimately do neither.

With Emma dead and Weston having fled to Mexico, the play ends as it had begun: with Ella and Wesley alone together on stage. Now, however, there is no family to save, no fate left to contend, nothing left to argue about. Instead, in a strangely harmonious moment, mother and son complete a story about a gigantic eagle begun by Weston at the very beginning of Act Three:

> WESTON   One time I was out in the fields doing the castrating. . . . Well, maybe I had a dozen spring ram lambs to do out there. . . . Well, I was working away out there when I feel this shadow cross over me . . . this giant eagle. . . . He was after these testes. . . . So I decided to oblige him . . . and threw a few on the shed roof . . . all of a sudden he comes. Just like a thunder clap. Blam!. . . . I had to stand up on that one. Somethin' brought me straight off the ground and I started yellin' my head off. . . . Cheerin for that eagle.[38]

What Weston neglects to mention, however, and what Ella and Wesley focus upon, is the arrival of a cat.

> ELLA   What happens next?
> WESLEY   A cat comes.

ELLA	That's right a big tom cat comes. Right out in the fields. And he jumps up on the roof to sniff around in all the entrails or what ever it was.
WESLEY	And that eagle comes down and picks up the cat in his talons and carries him screaming off into the sky.
ELLA	That's right. And they fight. They fight like crazy in the middle of the sky. The cat's tearing his chest out and the eagle's trying to drop him, but the cat won't let go because he knows if he falls he'll die.
WESLEY	And the eagle's being torn apart in midair. The eagle's trying to free himself from the cat, and the cat won't let go.
ELLA	And they come crashing down to earth. Both of them come crashing down. Like one whole thing.[39]

It is with this allegorical summation of the Tate family history that the play ends.[40] Whether it was some hereditary predeliction or free will (or for that matter, some ill-fated commingling of the two) that brought Weston "the eagle" to Ella "the cat," it was nonetheless this misalliance, this "cursed" partnership between two beasts ill-suited to the other's purposes and needs, which not only led to the destruction of both but also to the father's curse being passed down to the son and daughter they had engendered.

Notes

1. Lynda Hart quite accurately points out that Weston, by battering down "the barrier that insulates the family from the menace of the outside world . . . has reversed his role as protector and now represents a threatening intruder." Wesley, however, unlike his mother, Ella, refuses to acknowledge him as such. See *Sam Shepard's Metaphorical Stages* (Westport, Conn: Greenwood Press, 1987), 69.
2. Sam Shepard, *Curse of the Starving Class* in *Angel City, Curse of the Starving Class, & Other Plays* (New York: Urizen Books, 1976), 58.
3. Ibid.
4. Doris Auerbach, "Who Was Icarus's Mother?: The Powerless Mother Figures in the Plays of Sam Shepard," *Sam Shepard: A Casebook*, ed. Kimball King (New York: Garland Publishing, 1988), 55.
5. *Curse*, 58.
6. Ibid., 90.
7. Ibid.
8. Ibid., 65.
9. Ibid.
10. Ibid., 69.
11. Ibid.
12. Ibid., 64.
13. Ibid.
14. Ibid., 112.
15. Ibid.
16. Ibid., 66.
17. Ibid., 106–7.
18. "Even Minimal Shepard is Food for Thought," *New York Times*, 25 September 1983, sec. 2, 5.
19. *Curse*, 93.
20. Bonnie Marranca declares that "Shepard's magnificent obsession is the loss of individualism through control by unnameable forces." "Alphabetical Shepard: The Play of Words," *American Dreams: The Imagination of Sam Shepard*

(New York: Performing Arts Journal Publications, 1981), 18. And while one may argue that these "forces" are nameable (I believe I have, in fact, named them), one must nonetheless concede the overall accuracy of her assessment.

21 *Curse*, 59.

22 Ibid., 81.

23 One could argue that Wesley's attempts to keep the farm going are more symbolic than practical, and that while his repairs are piecemeal and do not significantly alter his family's predicament, they do nonetheless reveal both a willingness to address the situation (rather than flee it) and a belief that it can be corrected through right action.

24 *Curse*, 97–98.

25 Weston does not, however, articulate what this "right action" might be. It is clear that he has not solved this problem and hasn't even a vague theory (much less a concrete idea) as to how he might.

26 Lyons characterizes Shepard's "problematic father" as a "physically and mentally disabled man in deliberate self-exile, pursuing his . . . self-destructive course." See "Shepard's Family Trilogy and The Conventions of Modern Realism," *Rereading Shepard*, ed. Leonard Wilcox (New York: St. Martin's Press, 1993), 128.

27 *Curse*, 85.

28 Ibid., 87.

29 Ibid., 104.

30 "Alphabetical Shepard," 28.

31 *Curse*, 105.

32 Bonnie Marranca and Gautam Dasgupta, eds., *American Playwrights: A Critical Survey* (New York: Drama Books, 1981), 107.

33 *Curse*, 109.

34 Ibid.

35 Both Lynda Hart and Martin Tucker characterize Wesley's starvation as essentially spiritual in nature. What Emma and her brother truly seek is not food but rather a love that is supportive, tender, and readily accessible and that does not manifest itself alternately through indifference, antagonism, and abandonment. See Hart, *Sam Shepard's Metaphorical Stages*, 70, and Tucker, *Sam Shepard* (New York: Continuum, 1992), 124.

36 *Curse*, 112.

37 Ibid., 115.

38 Ibid., 102.

39 Ibid., 117–8.

40 Martin Tucker views the ending of *Curse* as "uncharacteristically resolute," while Bonnie Marranca conversely sees it as but another example of Shepard's "difficulty in ending his plays." See Tucker, *Sam Shepard*, 129, and Marranca, "Alphabetical Shepard," 19. Considering that Emma is dead, Weston has fled for good, and the now "cursed" Wesley and his mother face imminent dispossession, one finds Tucker's assessment to be the less disputable of the two. The family has indeed, to quote Ella's final words, "come crashing down. Like one whole thing."

Chapter Five

Buried Child; Buried Children

What most conspicuously distinguishes Shepard's Pulitzer Prize winning play, *Buried Child*, written in 1979, from his earlier father-son plays is its narrative—one which is paradoxically more conventional *and* more fantastic than its predecessors, and which will be discussed later at length. In many ways, however, the play is a pastiche of his previous work, utilizing many of the character types and thematic elements found in *The Holy Ghostly* and *Curse of the Starving Class*. As Bonnie Marranca succinctly puts it, "*Buried Child* doesn't move beyond the thematic territory of *Curse*."[1] Once again we find ourselves in a familial world where heredity ultimately prevails, where drunken fathers need alternately be protected by, and from, their sons, and where mothers must find whatever emotional sustenance they can outside the home.

The play begins with our being introduced to a lump beneath a brown blanket on a couch. The lump turns out to be Dodge, the family's patriarch. Rattily dressed and irascible in attitude, he reminds one immediately of an older, more physically incapacitated and consequently more infantile version of both Pop in *The Holy Ghostly* and Weston in *Curse of the Starving Class*. He is in fact so weak that he cannot physically flee his family and must escape as best he can via television and the whiskey he keeps hidden in the cushions of his couch.

For the first half of the first act, Dodge engages in a dialogue with his wife Halie. It is indicative of the extent to which their relationship has deteriorated that she remains upstairs and off-stage until the very end of their conversation. In this initial exchange Shepard focuses on Halie's sexual past, a subject which will prove increasingly significant as the play continues.

HALIE	I went once [to a horse race]. With a man.
DODGE	(*Mimicking her*) Oh, a "man."

. . . .

HALIE	A wonderful man. A breeder.
DODGE	A what?
HALIE	A breeder! A horse breeder! Thoroughbreds.

. . . .

DODGE   And he never laid a finger on you, I suppose. (*long silence*) Halie? *No answer. Long pause.*[2]

Having established Halie as a woman with sexual proclivities that extend beyond her husband, Shepard then introduces Tilden, the eldest of Dodge and Halie's three sons, a man in his forties about whom "something . . . is profoundly burnt-out and displaced."[3] Tilden enters carrying a huge armful of fresh corn which he claims he harvested out back. Dodge refutes this claim, stating "there is no corn out in back!" and that there hasn't been any there "since 1935!"[4] Tilden doggedly maintains, however, that there is "tons of it [out there]."[5] And so begins a pattern of interaction which pervades the entire play in which family members not only contradict the declarations and memories of the others, but often refute what they themselves have stated. Furthermore, these contradictions occur with such frequency that we soon find ourselves in an unsettling world where little is certain[6]—a world, in fact, infused with a sense of the fantastic.

In his book, *The Fantastic: A Structural Approach to a Literary Genre*, Tzvetan Todorov declares that the fantastic "requires the fulfillment of three conditions":

> First the text must oblige [the audience] to consider the world of the characters as a world of living persons and to hesitate *between a natural and supernatural explanation of the events described.*
>
> Secondly, this hesitation may also be experienced by a character. . . .
>
> Third, [the audience] must adopt a certain attitude with regard to the text: [they] will reject allegorical as well as "poetic interpretations. (emphasis mine)[7]

Accepting Todorov's criteria, one can then argue that *Buried Child* is, if not a wholly fantastic work, certainly one with recognizably fantastic elements. Tilden declares emphatically that the fields in back are now teeming with corn; but if so why, if as Halie and Dodge contend no corn has been planted for over forty years? The fact remains that neither parent goes outside to confirm Tilden's story, asserting instead that Tilden must have stolen the corn from a neighboring field. Consequently, the audience doesn't know what exactly to believe. Has some small miracle taken place or has Tilden lied in order to cover up his petty thievery? Or for that matter has he, being "burnt-out and displaced," merely confused his fields with those of someone else? Are we in a world where the inexplicable can be resolved eventually within the context of the natural world, or one where there are supernatural forces at play? Tilden's arrival on-stage has created a certain hesitancy, as defined by Todorov, within the audience's mind—one which intensifies right up to the play's final moments.

As Tilden settles down to shuck his corn and Dodge steals swigs from his bottle, Halie emerges from her bedroom, dressed funereally in a black dress and black-veiled hat. She is in mourning (nominally at least) for her dead son, Ansel, the one family member who

> would've taken care of us. . . . He would've seen to it that we were repaid. He was like that. He was a hero. Don't forget that. . . . Ansel could've been a great man. One of the greatest. I only regret that he didn't die in action. It's not fitting for a man like that to die in a motel room.[8]

Halie is also in some sense in mourning for her living sons, Tilden and Bradley. Neither one has lived up to her hopes. What Halie had expected was that her sons "would look after us."[9] She had believed initially that Bradley would be the one to take care of her and Dodge, but "Bradley can't hardly look after himself . . . after he lost his leg."[10] She then thought it would be Tilden who would take responsibility, "but then [he] turned out to be so much trouble."[11] Here again we recognize one of Shepard's recurring thematic motifs: the forfeiture of parental responsibility and the concomitant hope that the children will take control, that they will, in effect, become the parents and look after the apathetic self-seekers and tyrannical invalids who have given birth to them.

It becomes quickly apparent that unlike the son, Wesley, and the daughter, Emma, in *Curse of the Starving Class* who do attempt, however immaturely and ineffectually, to serve as the protectors and caretakers of their parents—the sons in *Buried Child* have neither the interest nor the ability to look after anyone. Before leaving the house to embark upon her great (and ludicrous) mission to have a statue built in Ansel's honor "with a basketball in one hand and a rifle in the other,"[12] Hallie repeatedly orders Dodge and Tilden to keep a close eye on one another. Soon after she departs, however, her admonitions are forgotten. After a brief exchange, Dodge falls asleep and Tilden, in a symbolic act (which Thomas Nash perceives as rich with mythological and religious overtones)[13] covers/buries his father beneath a sheet of corn husks. He then abandons Dodge and heads back out into the fields, stopping only to steal the last of his father's precious whiskey.[14]

With Dodge left couch-bound and unprotected, Bradley appears. If, as it is later implied, Tilden represents one aspect of the Oedipal impulse, the mother-seducer,[15] then it is Bradley who represents the other aspect: the father-slayer. Malevolent and physically imposing despite the loss of one leg, he attacks the sleeping Dodge with a pair of electric hair clippers, and in an act of retribution, whose cause we have yet to discover, shaves—or more precisely gouges—the hair off his father's head.

The second act begins with the arrival of Tilden's son, Vince, and his girlfriend, Shelly, the play's normative figures.[16] Vince had left home a number of years ago, and at this point Dodge, his grandfather, does not recognize him, mistaking him instead for Tilden—a fact which may further perplex and unsettle the audience, since from Shepard's descriptions they bear little physical resemblance to one another. Here again things appear to be bordering on the fantastic. Why is it that Dodge does not recognize his only living grandson, who, after all, has only been gone six years? Is he suffering from delirium? From senility? There is nothing we've witnessed previously that would indicate this. However great his physical incapacities, Dodge's mind appears clear and his memory strong. Consequently, we find ourselves involved in a seemingly inexplicable situation—one that, as Todorov states, is neither "poetic . . . [nor] allegorical"[17]—and where mysterious forces are again at work.

In an attempt to make contact, to somehow demonstrate his familial credentials, Vince finally asks Dodge about Halie, to which he replies:

> Don't worry about her. She won't be back for days. She says she'll be back but she won't be. (*he starts laughing*) There's life in the old girl yet. (*stops laughing*).[18]

Here, for a second time, Dodge alludes to Halie's sexuality. By reasserting this point—and by further emphasizing (however subtly) that Halie though in her mid-sixties still has the sexual wherewithal to go on "for days"—he is placing us on alert. Clearly, Halie has been a woman of great sexual power all her life and we now sense through these repeated allusions, that her erotic propensities are somehow central to the narrative which is about to unfold.

The narrative begins to assert itself more rapidly when Tilden returns once again from the fields, this time carrying an armful of carrots. No more capable of recognizing his son than was his father, he denies Vince's claim to be his son by declaring, "I had a son once but we buried him"[19] to which Dodge immediately and angrily responds: "You shut up about that! You don't know anything about that."[20]

It is at this moment that we become unequivocally aware that something has been hidden from us, that there may, in fact, exist real skeletons in the family closet. And it is upon this family secret and its eventual disclosure that the play's narrative in large measure hereafter focusses. Having hitherto resisted easy classification, Shepard's play has suddenly gone from being mysterious, in the deepest and most unsettling sense, to being a mystery—and a somewhat conventional and familiar one at that.[21] As Charles R. Lyons points out in his illuminating essay, "Shepard's Family Trilogy and the Conventions of Modern Realism," the use of "a retrospective structure"—which utilizes "the presence of an outsider" (in this case Shelly, the girlfriend)[22] who both "naturalizes the discussion of the past" and "questions those who inhabit the space," leading ultimately to the "narrative revelation" in which the familial past is finally unearthed (with usually tragic repercussions)—has long been a convention of realistic drama, beginning most notably with Ibsen and continuing through, among others, O'Neill, Miller (*All My Sons* and *Death of a Salesman*), and Albee (*Who's Afraid of Virginia Woolf?*).[23]

Having loudly proclaimed the existence of a family secret, Shepard further emphasizes its significance by having the group immediately redirect their attentions to safer, more mundane concerns: Dodge, with a singlemindedness reminiscent of *Endgame*'s Nagg, demands feebly that someone get him *his* "pap!"[24] (namely, a bottle of "Gold Star Sour Mash");[25] Tilden and Shelley begin to shear and cut up the carrots, while Vince perseveres unsuccessfully in his attempt to be recognized by his father and grandfather.

Eventually, Vince agrees to go off and fetch his grandfather his whiskey, and it is in his absence, with Dodge glued to the TV set, that Tilden again obliquely alludes to the family secret:

TILDEN   There are certain things I can't tell you. . . .
. . . .
SHELLY   Well, you can tell me anything you want to.
TILDEN   I can?
SHELLY   Sure.

TILDEN	It might not be very nice.
SHELLY	That's all right. I've been around.
TILDEN	It might be awful.[26]

They continue, however, to converse, and when Shelly demonstrates her trustworthiness by allowing this man-child to stroke and finally to hold her fur coat, Tilden begins to confide more freely:

TILDEN	If I told you something you wouldn't understand it. . . . .
SHELLY	Like what?
TILDEN	Like a baby. Like a tiny little baby. . . . If I told you you'd make me give your coat back.
SHELLY	I won't. I promise. Tell me.
TILDEN	I can't. Dodge won't let me.
SHELLY	He won't hear you. It's okay.
TILDEN	We had a baby. He did. Dodge did. . . . Little baby. Dodge killed it. . . . Dodge drowned it.[27]

Dodge, suddenly aware of what Tilden's been saying, struggles desperately to get off the couch. He eventually succeeds and begins to move painfully towards his son. Soon however, the effort proves too great and Dodge collapses onto the floor, "moving his lips silently as though talking to someone invisible."[28] It is at this moment that Bradley reappears. Having spoken the unspeakable, Tilden soon flees, leaving Shelly to face Bradley alone.

It is in these, the concluding moments of the second act, that Bradley reveals the true magnitude of his malevolence; it is not enough for him to symbolically destroy his father, he must revenge himself upon his brother as well. Functioning as both Oedipus and Cain, he not only "buries" his still-breathing father (and in a far more brutish and triumphant manner than had Tilden),[29] but symbolically rapes Shelly[30] by forcing her to open her mouth, and leave it open, as he sticks in his fingers.[31]

Unlike Acts One and Two, which take place in the rain, Shepard opens Act Three with the sun shining as if to prepare us for the illuminations to come. Bradley, having completed his Oedipal triumph by usurping his father's couch and blanket, thus claiming for himself the role of the tyrannical invalid, now sleeps, his wooden leg resting near his head. Shelly, seemingly unaffected by the events of the night before, emerges from the kitchen with some beef bouillon for Dodge, who is once again his cantankerous self. Having been upstairs studying the photographs in Halie's bedroom, and having noticed one photo in particular in which a young Halie is "looking down at a baby like it was somebody else's. Like it didn't belong to her,"[32] Shelly asks Dodge if "Tilden was telling the truth . . . about the baby?"[33] Dodge does not answer, wondering instead as to Tilden's whereabouts. At that moment, Halie is heard returning and Dodge suddenly and inexplicably turns frantic:

DODGE   (*To SHELLY in a heavy whisper pulling his coat around him*)
         Don't leave me alone now! Promise me. Don't go off and leave me alone. I need somebody here with me. Tilden's gone now and I need someone. Don't leave me! Promise!
SHELLY   (*sitting*) I won't.[34]

Halie enters the living room, laughing flirtatiously, accompanied by Father Dewis who carries a bouquet of yellow roses. Despite her having spent the night with a man somewhere other than in her own home, Halie, upon seeing Shelly—and Bradley's unattached wooden leg—assumes (rather theatrically) the role of the scandalized matriarch:

HALIE   What in the name of Judas Priest is going on in this home . . . you can't leave this house for a second without the Devil blowing though the front door![35]

Within seconds, however, Halie drops that role in favor of a more punitive one. Flaunting her intimacies with Father Dewis, she gigglingly reaches into the minister's pockets for what's left of the whiskey the two spent the night sharing. Shepard never makes it absolutely clear whether Halie merely flirted and drank with Father Dewis all night, or seduced him outright. Nevertheless by the time she arrives home, no longer dressed in funereal black but in "bright yellow,"[36] she has achieved what was ostensibly her goal: namely, to have a statue built in honor of Ansel.

It is Halie's conviction that "we can't stop believing. We just end up dying if we stop"[37]—even if what one believes in is a complete and utter lie. By honoring Ansel, a man who we were told died in a motel room never having seen military action, and who furthermore (as Bradley points out) "never played basketball,"[38] Halie is attempting to recast her family publicly as not merely admirable in a conventional sense, but as extraordinary (and, as such, beyond suspicion). Indeed, one may argue that the degree and manner of this tribute is a clear measure of just how deeply Halie needs to hide the disgrace to which she has contributed. Hoping to bury the family secret once and for all, she oversees the building of a monument to an idealized son who never existed, and who in fact brought no more honor upon her family than did Tilden or Bradley.

What Halie has in actuality presided over is a family of stunted children, men who despite their size and age have, as the result of circumstances, either never grown up or, like Dodge, reverted back into children in their old age. What gives Shepard's title its extraordinary metaphoric resonance is not the fact that there exists a dead baby buried somewhere in the woods (who may or may not be unearthed), but rather that there exists within each living member of the family a buried child who sooner or later re-emerges. With Dodge and Bradley,[39] it is physical incapacitation which calls the child forth, while with Tilden, the most consistently childlike of the three, it is guilt, failure, and institutionalization.

Thematic considerations aside, it should be reiterated that *Buried Child* is a mystery which does center on a child whose death up to now has only been partially explained. We know from Tilden that there was in fact a baby, that Dodge drowned it and buried it, and that the family was able keep this fact from the police. What has yet to be explained is Dodge's motive. What was it about Dodge and/or this baby that compelled him to kill it?

To call *Buried Child* a mystery is not, however, to suggest that it adheres strictly to the genre's conventions. Shepard is an iconoclastic playwight, after all, who has publicly declared his disdain for neat, conclusive endings.

> I think it's a cheap trick to resolve things. It's a complete lie to make resolutions. I've always felt that particularly in the theatre, when everything's tied up at the end with a neat little ribbon and you're delivered this package. You walk out of the theatre feeling that everything's resolved and you know what the play's about. So what?[40]

Hence, it seems quite conceivable that when Shepard has Dodge mock Shelly for thinking "she's going to uncover the truth of the matter. Like a detective or something,"[41] he is simultaneously addressing and mocking the audience's desire for the narrative to follow a familiar path, to be a mystery like other mysteries, in which the questions the plot poses are in the end logically and satisfyingly answered. What Shepard does instead is utilize certain genre conventions only to then thwart the expectations that those conventions call forth.

This is exemplied in the play's moment of revelation, the moment when Dodge finally confesses both his crime and its motives. Unlike more conventional mysteries where, say, a clever interrogator goads and/or tricks the criminal into admitting his guilt (perhaps by producing some unexpected and irrefutable piece of evidence), here there is only Shelly, an utterly ineffectual seeker of truth whose demand to know meets not only with close-lipped defiance (Halie and Bradley) but derisive laughter (Dodge).

Immediately thereafter, Shepard challenges our expectations once more. Having easily weathered Shelly's attempt to "get it [the secret] out of us,"[42] Dodge suddenly, and one could argue almost capriciously, agrees, despite the imprecations of Bradley and Halie, to decribe both the murder and the events leading up to it.

DODGE   . . . Halie has this kid. This baby boy. . . . This one hurt real bad. Almost killed her, but she had it anyway. It lived, see. It lived. It wanted to grow up in this family. . . . It wanted to pretend that I was its father. She [Halie] wanted me to believe in it. Even when everyone around us knew. Everyone. All our boys knew. Tilden knew.
HALIE   You shut up! Bradley, make him shut up!
BRADLEY   I can't.
DODGE   Tilden was the one who knew. Better than any of us. . . . We couldn't let a thing like that continue. . . . It made everything we'd accomplished look like it was nothin'. Everything was cancelled out by this one mistake. This one weakness.
SHELLY   So you killed him?
DODGE   I killed it. I drowned it. Just like the runt of the litter. Just drowned it.[43]

Although Dodge does not confess outright that Tilden impregnated Halie, he does state quite clearly that he himself was not the baby's father. Moreover, if we examine Dodge's monologue, and its emphasis on Tilden knowing what happened "better than any of us," in conjunction with Tilden's earlier statement that *he* "had a son once but we buried him,"[44] the incestuous nature of his relationship with Halie becomes readily apparent.[45]

Having had Dodge confess his crime and in so doing reveal the family secret, which in a conventional, realistic mystery would serve as its denouement and signal its impending end, Shepard then proceeds to shift the play's tone and focus altogether by reintroducing Vince. Outraged at having been not only ignored but unrecognized, he returns home drunk and violent.[46] Tearing the porch door off its hinges (a la Weston at the beginning of *Curse*), he declares himself "a murderer . . . [capable of devouring] whole families in a single gulp"[47] and begins hurling empty whiskey bottles against the front of the house. Ironically, it is this degenerate display which allows him at last to be recognized as a member of the family, first by Dodge and then by Halie. Furthermore, as Vince continues smashing things and uttering idiocies, going so far as to strike out at Bradley with a bottle, his grandparents, rather than drawing back, embrace him all the more completely. Halie suddenly sees in him what she's been searching for in each of her sons: namely, "a guardian angel" who'll "watch over us";[48] while Dodge, having confessed his sins and now near death, names Vince his successor, bequeathing him "the house . . . all the furnishings, accoutrements and paraphernalia therein."[49]

In the face of such overwhelming reacceptance, Vince, much to Shelly's astonishment, decides to stay. Knowing full well that this means the end of their involvement, he recounts, by way of explanation, his experience while driving the night before:

> I could see my face in the windshield. My face. My eyes. I studied my face. Studied everything about it. As though I was looking at another man. As though I could see his whole race behind him. Like a mummy's face. I saw him dead and alive at the same time. In the same breath . . . . and every breath marked him. Marked him forever without him knowing. And then his face changed. His face became his father's face. Same bones. Same eyes. Same nose. Same breath. And his father's face changed into his grandfather's face. And it went on like that. Changing. Clear on to faces I'd never seen before but still recognized. Still recognized the bones underneath. The eyes. The breath. The mouth.[50]

Here, as in *Curse of The Starving Class*, Shepard asserts the power of heredity, of familial alliances to prevail over all others. But unlike in the earlier play, where heredity is seen by its characters as a "poison," a ruinous power to which one must eventually succumb despite all of one's attempts to do otherwise, in *Buried Child* it is seen, by Vince at least, in comparatively neutral terms. As far as the family heir is concerned, heredity is not something that one need fear, or try to escape, but merely an elementary fact of life to be accepted and, ideally, embraced.

It is possible, however, to view Vince's comparatively benign view of heredity ironically, as, in fact, the result of simple ignorance. Absent during the confessions of both his father and grandfather, he is consequently unaware that his is a family where fathers murder children and mothers sleep with their sons. Much like Weston in *Curse* who "only recognized *his* father's poison" when he saw himself "infected with it,"[51] Vince has yet to discover the degree to which he is cursed.

In fact, as the play moves briskly towards its conclusion, it is clear that Vince sees himself as the triumphant successor, the man who will lead his family proudly forward. Having broken off with Shelly, he continues to clean house, first by expelling Bradley, and then by placing the bouquet of yellow roses brought by Father Dewis atop the chest of his now dead grandfather.

Lynda Hart and Henry Schvey (among others), however, contest the idea that Vince is the "family savior"[52] whose victory signals a new future for the family, by pointing to a subsequent stage direction.

> VINCE . . . *then lays down on the sofa, arms folded behind his head, staring at the ceiling. His body is in the same relationship to* DODGE'S.[53]

It is their argument that by placing Vince in the identical posture as his dead grandfather, Shepard shows that though one generation has supplanted another, little, in fact, has changed.[54] Dodge, the child-killer, may have died, but another drunken, violent man capable of attacking his own family has taken his place. In *Buried Child*, as in *Curse of the Starving Class*, history is shown to be circular, rather than linear, with the future being but the past reborn.

Shepard further undermines any sense of familial regeneration in the play's concluding moments. As the lights begin to dim on Vince and Dodge, Halie, now upstairs, declares:

> Tilden was right about the corn you know. I've never seen such corn. . . . Tall as a man already. . . . It's a paradise out there. . . . A miracle. I've never seen it like this. Maybe the rain did something. Maybe it was the rain.[55]

In corroborating Tilden's earlier pronouncements, Halie reasserts the play's fantastic aspect and, by extension, her expectation that things shall end happily. If this is a world where paradises can manifest themselves inexplicably and without warning, then families too can reblossom, no matter how abominable their past behavior. It is at Halie's moment of high optimism, when the future seems assured, when nature itself appears to be heralding Vince's return and the family's continuance, that Shepard, via Tilden's reappearance, draws us back to the inexpiable past. Re-emerging from the fields, "his arms . . . covered with mud,"[56] Tilden returns this time, not with vegetables, but with a far more grisly offering: the remains of the buried child. He has literally unearthed the family's "curse," which though long hidden is shown to be ultimately inevasible. Holding the baby whom his father had murdered and whom he himself had sired, Tilden silently and ominously mounts the stairs towards his mother-wife, moving towards a moment when Halie, ever ready to dismiss the past, to obliterate it in one way or another, will be forced to confront it in its most concrete form.

Notes

1. Bonnie Marranca and Gautam Dasgupta, eds., *American Playwrights: A Critical Survey* (New York: Drama Books, 1981), 109.

2. Sam Shepard, *Buried Child* in *Buried Child, Seduced, Suicide in B Flat* (New York: Urizen Books, 1979), 13–14.

3. Ibid., 16.

4. Ibid., 17

5. Ibid.

6. Charles Lyons confirms this assessment, stating "Shepard's dialogue refuses to expose unequivocally the precise coordinates of the [family's] past." See "Shepard's Family Trilogy and the Conventions of Modern Realism," *Rereading Shepard*, ed. Leonard Wilcox (New York: St. Martin's Press, 1993), 121.

7. *The Fantastic: A Structural Approach to a Literary Genre* (Ithaca, NY: Cornell University Press, 1975) 33.

8. *Buried Child*, 20.

9. Ibid.

10. Ibid.

11. Ibid.

12. Ibid., 21.

13. In his essay on the mythological aspects of *Buried Child*, Thomas Nash points out that the play's plot "is a modern version of the central theme of Western mythology, the death and rebirth of the Corn King," and that Tilden's tender burial of Dodge beneath the corn husks suggests "Dodge's symbolic role as the Corn King in the winter of his life." See "Sam Shepard's Buried Child: The Ironic Use of Folklore," *Essays on American Drama: Williams, Miller, Albee, and Shepard*, ed. Dorothy Parker (Toronto: University of Toronto Press, 1987), 203, 206. For a more detailed discussion of the Corn King myth see James Frazier's *The New Golden Bough*, ed. Theodor H. Gaster (New York: Criterion Books, 1959), 425–444.

14. Henry Schvey contends that Tilden "has been reduced to a state of childlike dependency by the machinations of the patriarchal Dodge." See "A Worm in the Wood: The Father-Son Relationship in the Plays of Sam Shepard," *Modern Drama*, 36 (March 1993), 22. It should be pointed out, however, that while Tilden is indeed "child-like" and dependent on his parents for food and shelter, he is also, in certain respects, his own man. Halie admits as much when she states that Tilden "never listens to me." (*Buried Child*, 24). Nor

does he obey his father with any regularity. Despite Dodge's plea that Tilden "watch out for me. Get me things when I need them," (*Buried Child*, 26), Tilden comes and goes as he pleases, steals his father's whiskey, and later, in the face of his father's long-standing command to keep silent, reveals the existence of the family secret to Shelly.

15 Freud defines the Oedipal complex as a twofold phenomena in which the son wishes not only to kill the father but marry the mother. Sigmund Freud, *Introductory Lectures on Psychoanalysis*, trans. and ed. James Strachey (New York: W.W. Norton, 1966), 207. *Buried Child* is the first of Shepard's father-son plays to deal with the latter aspect of this complex. In the plays we previously analyzed, Shepard focused exclusively on the son's desire to destroy the father and in so doing, break free of him.

16 Bruce J. Mann rightfully makes the point that "Vince and Shelly are normal when we first meet them, and . . . Shelly remains so. But Vince metamorphoses later." See "Character Behavior and the Fantastic in Sam Shepard's *Buried Child*," *Sam Shepard: A Casebook*, ed. Kimball King (New York: Garland, 1988), 83.

17 *The Fantastic*, 33.

18 *Buried Child*, 33.

19 Ibid., 37.

20 Ibid., 48.

21 One might argue, hopefully without appearing too cynical, that it is the very conventionality of *Buried Child*'s narrative which explains, in large measure, the play's critical and popular success.

22 Both Jane Ann Crum and Lynda Hart view Shelly as the character whose perspective most precisely represents that of the audience. Crum declares that "Shelly serves as our mediator in the search for meaning and allows the audience an outlet for its frustrations as that meaning is continually denied." Similarly, Hart states that Shelly functions "as an objective presence . . . with no familial ties whose point of view provides the audience with a perspective from which they can judge the reality of this family's life." See Crum, "Notes on *Buried Child*," *Sam Shepard: A Casebook*, ed. Kimball King (New York: Garland, 1988), 76, and Hart, *Sam Shepard's Metaphorical Stages* (Westport, Conn: Greenwood Press, 1987), 77–78.

23 Charles R. Lyons, "Shepard's Family Trilogy and the Conventions of Modern Realism," 118–123.

24 Samuel Beckett, *Endgame* (New York: Grove Press, 1958), 9.

25 *Buried Child*, 44.

26 Ibid., 45.

27 Ibid., 47.

28 Ibid., 48.

29 Rather than cover him gently with corn husks, Bradley (wearing a cruel triumphant smile) "buries" Dodge by holding Shelly's coat high over his head and then tossing it down over the face of his comatose father.

30 Bradley misperceives Shelly as being involved with, and therefore an extension of, Tilden. Hence by violating her orally with his finger, a phallic substitute, he believes he is attacking his brother.

31 Jim McGhee points out how clearly the conclusion of Act Two mirrors that of Act One, stating that "each act ends with Dodge in a posture of helpless defeat." *True Lies: The Architecture of the Fantastic in the Plays of Sam Shepard* (New York: Peter Lang, 1993), 93. It should also be noted that while in that "posture" Dodge is subjected to a symbolic burial and that both acts also end with Bradley's symbolic emasculation of the two men who have deprived him of his mother's favors.

32 *Buried Child*, 52.

33 Ibid., 53.

34 Ibid., 56.

35 Ibid., 57.

36 Ibid.

37 Ibid., 60.

38 Ibid., 59.

39 It is most telling that when Bradley, that colossus of Oedipal rage, is both without his wooden leg and is denied his father's blanket, he whimpers and calls out to his mother like a small boy.

40 Sam Shepard, interview by Amy Lippman, "Rhythms and Truth: An Interview with Sam Shepard," *American Theatre*, 1, no. 1. (1984).

41 *Buried Child*, 63.

42 Ibid.

43 Ibid., 65.

44 Ibid., 37.

45 Here again we see Shepard expressing two of his more familiar themes: the inconstancy of familial roles and the Oedipal triumph of son over father. But what distinguishes *Buried Child* from *The Holy Ghostly* and *The Tooth of Crime* is that in the latter works, the son's victory was achieved through the death of the father, who, being a figure of some power, needed to be over-

come by force; whereas in *Buried Child* it is achieved sexually via the seduction of the mother.

46   Jim McGhee contends that 1) the "transformation of character . . . [is one of] the techniques of the fantastic," and 2) such a "transformation" is "most evident in Vince." *True Lies*, 96. One can, however, also view Vince's behavioral metamorphosis in realistic terms, namely he is roaring drunk.

47   *Buried Child*, 67.

48   Ibid., 69.

49   Ibid.

50   Ibid., 70.

51   *Curse of the Starving Class, in Angel City, Curse of the Starving Class and Other Plays* (New York: Urizen Books), 87.

52   Marranca and Dasgupta, *American Playrights*, 109

53   *Buried Child*, 72.

54   Hart declares that by "positioning himself on the sofa in Dodge's place . . . his body symmetrically mimicking the position of Dodge's corpse . . . Vince [reveals that he] cannot transcend the past, the inexorable power of the patriarchy claims him," while Schvey states that "in this tableau vivant, Shepard clearly indicates that Vince is not reawakened but entombed by the poisons of the past, just as the position of his body suggests death not life." See Hart, *Sam Shepard's Metaphorical Stages*, 85, and Schvey, "A Worm in the Wood," 24.

55   *Buried Child*, 72.

56   Ibid.

Chapter Six

True West: The Spell of the Hermit King

In marked contrast to Shepard's earlier father-son plays, the father in *True West* never appears on stage. Despite his absence, a number of critics nonetheless regard the old man as central to the play's dramatic action. Charles R. Lyons views the father as a figure "significant [to the] narrative;"[1] while Martin Tucker takes things a step further, positioning the old man at the very "apex of the [familial] triad."[2] Lynda Hart, in her essay "Realism Revisited" puts things even more precisely, stating that while the play's protagonists, the brothers Austin and Lee, attempt to "disassociate themselves from their father . . . in reality, [they] cannot escape . . . [his] influence."[3] Of the three aforementioned critics, I find myself agreeing most with Professor Hart. It is my contention that it is the father, despite his absence, who dominates the play's action. Living alone in the desert, a toothless, ill-tempered old man consumed by drink, he nevertheless rules over his sons' lives like a hermit king, alternately driving them out of the wilderness and summoning them back.

Of the two sons, it is Lee who more closely resembles the father. Like "the old man," he is ill-kempt, belligerent, and an incessant drinker.[4] Moreover, he too is something of a desert rat, having fled society, its judgements and constraints, in favor of a more solitary—and consequently more autonomous—life in the wild.

Despite these obvious similarities, Lee is quick to make clear that he is not a mere rubber stamp of his father and is not to be treated as such. Hence, when Austin offers him money (as he has so often done to their father) Lee explodes:

> Don't you say that to me! . . . .You may be able to git away with that with the old man. Get him tanked for a week! Buy him off

with yer Hollywood blood money, but not me! I can git my own own money my own way. Big money![5]

Although having emulated his father (in a great many ways), Lee clearly regards the old man with intense ambivalence. He sees him essentially as a weakling susceptible to being bought off—a drunkard whose need for drink has destroyed his principles and pride, and turned him into a whore. Conversely, Lee views himself as self-sufficient, as the master of his domain, regardless of how unsavory that domain may be.

Lee, as we discover early in the play, is a burglar and thief. His ostensible reason for coming to southern California is not to visit his mother (who, as it turns out, is away on a trip) but rather to burglarize her suburban neighborhood—one which he has cased in advance of the play's action and found to be easy pickings.

> This is a great neighborhood. Lush. Good class a' people. Not too many dogs . . . [they're] never gonna know. All they know is somethin's missing. That's all . . . . Nobody's gonna know.[6]

Like the Western bandits of old, Lee's modus operandi is to swoop down upon an unsuspecting community, plunder it, and then vanish back to his desert hideaway.

And yet, as proud as Lee is of his abilities, and as successful as he has been in plying his trade, Lee is nonetheless disenchanted with the life he has led, with having followed for so long his father's path. What this criminal outcast yearns for is the security and respectability of the middle class. Lee reveals as much in a description of one of the homes he's cased:

> [It was] like a paradise. Kinda' place that sorta kills ya' inside. Warm yellow lights. Mexican tile all around. . . . Blond people movin' in and outa' rooms. talkin' to each other. (pause) *Kinda place you wish you'd sorta grew up in, ya' know.* (emphasis mine).[7]

Hence, as the play unfolds and as his rivalry with his younger brother intensifies, Lee's true ambitions—though never explicitly declared—come to the fore. He may have come to southern California merely to loot a few houses, but as new possiblities present themselves, he sees the chance for a new life. Suddenly, the opportunity has arisen for him to be both Cain and Christ, to usurp Austin's successful position in the world and, in so doing, save his father from utter dissolution.

Austin is the brother, or so it initially seems, who has truly broken free of "the old man's" spell. A respected screenwriter and family man, with a wife and children, neither contemptuous by nature nor a drunkard, he has accomplished what so many of Shepard's sons (i.e., Tilden and Vincent in *Buried Child*, and Wesley in *Curse of the Starving Class*) have attempted and failed; namely, he has gotten beyond the familial call of the wild and entrenched himself in the world at large.

As the first scene begins, Lee is seated at their vacationing mother's kitchen table observing his younger brother at work.[8] Forced to acknowledge, on some level, his own socioeconomic inferiority, he quickly counters, accusing Austin of arrogance:

LEE	Yer line a' work. . . . You probably think that I'm not fully able to comprehend somethin' like that, huh?
AUSTIN	Like what?
LEE	That stuff yer doin'. That art. You know. Whatever you call it.
AUSTIN	It's just a little research.
LEE	You may not know it but I did a little art myself once.
AUSTIN	You did?
LEE	Yeah! I did some a' that. I fooled around with it. No future in it.
AUSTIN	What'd you do?
LEE	Never mind what I did! Just never mind about that. (Pause) It was ahead of its time.[9]

In one fell swoop, Lee establishes himself both as Austin's equal ("I did art") and his superior, for unlike his brother, he recognizes art's essential pointlessness ("that stuff. . . . [There's] No future in it"). This accusation of arrogance clearly strikes a familiar chord in Austin for he immediately directs their conversation towards their father: "So, you went to see the old man, huh?"[10]

In Scene Two, Lee persists in his attacks. Despite the fact that his brother continually defers to him, downplaying both his work and his degree of success, Lee is driven to reasssert his superiority—and by extension his father's:

LEE	You never had any more on the ball than I did. . . . In fact I probably got a wider range a' choices than you do, come to think of it.
AUSTIN	I wouldn't doubt it.
LEE	In fact I been inside some pretty classy places in my time. And I never even went to an Ivy league school either.[11]

As the scene proceeds, it becomes increasingly apparent that there is nothing Austin can say or do to assuage his brother's insecurities. Yet as long as Austin continues to acquiesce, some modicum of peace is maintained. Late in the scene, however, circumstances force Austin to assert himself. Having scheduled, previous to Lee's arrival, an in-house script meeting with an important Hollywood producer, Saul Kimmer, he asks, rather reasonably, that he be allowed the place to himself for a few hours. His brother, however, ever sensitive to any sign of disrespect, regards this request as an insult, an overt confirmation of his essential inferiority.

> LEE   Yer afraid I'll embarass ya' huh?
> AUSTIN I'm not afraid you'll embarass me!
> . . . . .
> LEE   You want me to just git lost, huh? Take a hike? Is that it? Pound the pavement for a fews hours while you bullshit yer way into a million bucks.[12]

Eventually Lee, having negotiated the rights to Austin's car, agrees to go. But before he does, he makes it clear that a real battle is imminent:

> Hey, ya' know, if that uh—story of yours doesn't go over with the guy—tell him I got a couple a' projects' he might be interested in. Real commercial. Full a' suspense. True-to-life stuff.[13]

The brothers' competition begins in earnest in Scene Three. Conveniently arriving home (with a stolen television in tow) in the middle of Austin and Kimmer's conference, Lee quickly gets the producer to consider a story idea of his—one which Austin is enlisted to flesh out—and join him the next day in a game of golf. That night marks the beginning of the brothers' collaboration and a shift in the hierarchical nature of their relationship. Now it is Lee who is the artist in control and Austin his more experienced subordinate. As they argue over the story's implausibilities, Lee imagines what he would do with the money if it were sold:

> LEE   We could get the old man outa' hock then.
> AUSTIN Maybe.
> LEE   Whatdya' mean, maybe?
> AUSTIN I mean it might take more than money.
> LEE   You were just tellin' me it'd change my whole life around. Why wouldn't it change him?

AUSTIN	He's different.
LEE	Oh, he's a different ilk, huh?
AUSTIN	He's not gonna change. Let's leave the old man out of it.
LEE	That's right. He's not gonna change but I will. I'll just turn myself right inside out. I could be just like you then, huh?[14]

In this exchange, Lee contradicts his earlier claim to being unlike his father. Clearly, he views himself and his father as being, in essence, identical—and therefore equally susceptible to change—and is insulted that Austin would view them otherwise. Furthermore, in planning to use *his* screenwriting monies to save his father, Lee defines himself as his brother's antithesis. He is the good son who will not disavow and abandon his curse-ridden father, as Austin has done, but instead will transform him.

This notion of Austin as the fleeing Judas pursued by Lee, the retributive agent of his betrayed father, is none-too-subtly reflected in the tale Lee is trying to sell. Ostensibly a Western "based on a true story,"[15] in which one cowboy, having slept with the wife of another cowboy, is chased by the latter down through Texas and into Mexico, it is in actuality a family parable chronicling Austin's flight from his father and the father's attempt, via his surrogate, to hunt him down and exact his revenge.[16]

By the fifth scene, Lee has seemingly sealed his victory. Having hustled Kimmer on the golf course, he has not only manipulated the producer into optioning his story and promising him a big advance, but he also has convinced Kimmer to set aside a huge sum of money in trust for his father—a trust that Lee himself will administer.[17] Moreover, it has been decided that Austin is to discontinue work on the script he's been developing and adapt Lee's story instead. Outraged at having his work dismissed and his position so suddenly and unjustly usurped, Austin's first impulse is to escape back to the wilderness:

AUSTIN	Just give me my keys! I gotta' take a drive. I gotta' get out of here for awhile.
LEE	Where you gonna go, Austin?
AUSTIN	(Pause) I might just drive out to *the desert* for a while. I gotta' think. (emphasis mine)[18]

Lee, however, is unwilling to give him the keys. Fearing that Austin might take off altogether, and needing him, in both a practical and psychological sense, to collaborate in his own undoing, he blocks his brother's escape, telling him that:

> You can think here just as good. This is the perfect set-up for thinkin'. We got some writin' to do here, boy. Now let's just have us a little toast. Relax. We're partners now.[19]

But in the sixth scene, Austin decides, uncharacteristically, not to participate in this "partnership." Having been betrayed so cavalierly, he can no longer suppress the darker, more belligerent side of himself. Rather than deal with this difficult situation diplomatically (as he would have in the past), Austin instead defies and insults those responsible. In a self-destructive demonstration worthy of his father,[20] Austin not only refuses Kimmer's offer of three hundred thousand dollars, but seals his professional demise by denouncing the producer as "dried up" and "a fool."[21] Suddenly unemployed, and quite possibly blackballed, Austin has taken his first real steps back toward the world he had fled, a world where one lives, however marginally, by one's wits, and where failure and freedom are extricably linked.

Having observed the competition, the psychological makeup of its two combatants, and its outcome, one cannot help but note how similar it is to that between Hoss and the unheralded Gypsy, Crow, in *The Tooth of Crime*. In both plays, an underdog unencumbered by moral restraints triumphantly does battle with his more successful, rule-dominated opponent on the latter's home turf. Furthermore, in winning, the underdog lays claim to his enemy's wealth and status, and having thereby stripped his opponent of his identity, leaves him with little recourse but to attempt to return to his roots—which in the case of Austin means a psycho-spiritual return to his father.

What distinguishes the two plays, however, is that Lee's victory is nowhere nearly as complete as that of Crow's, nor is Austin's defeat as devastating as that of Hoss's. This is made immediately apparent at the beginning of Scene Seven. The scene begins just as Scene One had, with the two brothers sitting across from one another at the kitchen table. Now, however, their roles are reversed: it is Lee who is struggling to write despite the interruptions of his drunk[22] and slyly malicious younger brother. Confident at first that he could "have this thing done in a night,"[23] Lee eventually admits to being utterly at a loss as to how to proceed:

> LEE   Just help me a little with the characters, all right? You know how to do it, Austin.
> AUSTIN   (On floor, laughing) The characters!
> LEE   Yeah. You know. The way they talk and stuff. I can hear it in my head but I can't get it down on paper.

AUSTIN   What characters?
LEE   The guys. The guys in the story.[24]

Despite Lee's continued pleas, and subsequent offers of shared screen credit, money, and the promise to "never bother ya again,"[25] Austin refuses to help. Having been humiliated, it is now his turn to exact revenge.

> Yer on your own now old buddy. You bulldogged yer way into contention. Now you gotta carry it through. . . . You don't come up with a winner on your first time out they just cut off your head. They don't give ya a second chance ya' know.[26]

Furthermore, Austin, who is now so transformed as to actually "sound . . . like the old man,"[27] has still other acts of vengeance planned. It is not enough for Lee to fail as a writer, he must also be defeated on *his* home turf. Hence, Austin sets out to burglarize the neighborhood and prove himself his brother's criminal equal. But before he leaves, Austin tells a story Lee had never before heard, involving himself and his father and his father's false teeth.

> I go out there and I take him out for a nice Chinese dinner. But he doesn't eat. All he wants to do is drink Martinis outa' plastic cups. And he takes his [false] teeth out and lays 'em on the table 'cause he can't stand the feel of 'em. And we ask the waitress for one a' those doggie bags to take the Chop Suey home in. So he drops his teeth in the doggie bag along with the Chop Suey. And then we hit all the bars up and down the highway. Says he wants to introduce me to all his buddies. And in one a' those bars up and down the highway, he left the doggie bag with his teeth lying in the Chop Suey.[28]

Lynda Hart declares Austin's story to be an expression of "the anger and resentment he feels toward his father."[29] It is arguable, however, that quite the opposite is true, that this anecdote, sad and ridiculous as it is, shows Austin and his father in a new light, free of the contempt and blame which had characterized their earlier meetings. Here the old man appears not only to accept Austin but to regard him with pride (he wanted "to introduce me to all his buddies"). Suddenly it seems that the father's affections are not so one-sided after all, and that there exists the possibility that another—and perhaps the most significant—aspect of Lee's identity may be usurped: that of favorite son.[30]

Scene Eight takes place the following morning, with Lee chopping away at his typewriter with a golf club in utter frustration. Having failed in his attempt to both supplant his brother and realize his own dreams of middle-class respectability, Lee angrily declares "this is the last time I live with people, boy!"[31] His plan now is to return to the desert and his father. Austin, on the other hand, is busy celebrating his criminal achievements. As we view a long line of stolen toasters all cooking away, it is clear that he has succeeded in burglarizing not one home, as had Lee, but many. Having so proven his courage and competance, Austin feels himself capable of surviving no matter what the circumstances, and asks Lee if he might accompany him into the desert.

Once more power has shifted hands. Having had his own pleas for help roughly rebuffed in the preceding scene, Lee is quick to turn Austin down. Whether it is because (as he states) that Austin "wouldn't last a day out there,"[32] or whether it is because he fears, subliminally, that he might, Lee is intent on returning alone.

Austin, however, will not be refused. He confesses that he has been as dissatisfied with the life he's chosen as Lee has been with his, and that what he yearns for most is not money and worldly success but the harsh autonomy of life in the wilderness from which he once fled.[33]

> LEE   What're you, crazy or somethin'? You went to college. Here you are down here, rollin' in bucks. Floatin' up and down in elevators. And you wanna' learn how to live on a desert!
>
> AUSTIN I do Lee, I really do. There's nothin' down here for me. There never was. . . . There's nothin' real down here. . . . Least of all me![34]

Lee regards his brother's romanticization of desert life as madness, and in perhaps his only moment of true honesty, makes it clear why he and his father are desert rats.

> Hey, do you actually think I chose to live out in the middle a' nowhere? Do ya? Ya' think it's some kinda' philosophical decision I took or somethin'? I'm livin' out there 'cause I can't make it here![35]

Austin, however, remains undissuaded. He has his own reasons for venturing out into the desert. Unlike his brother and father, who have been relegated to a life in the wilderness by their own social inadequacies, Austin has been able to "make it here"—but at what he considers too great a price. By returning both physically and psycho-spiritually to the world of his father, Austin sees the chance to rediscover his authenticity,[36] to experience a more primal reality, and to finally transcend his need for societal acceptance. Hence, he stubbornly persists in his pleas until Lee eventually relents—but only after he (Lee) strikes what he ironically terms a "little trade":[37]

> You write me up this screenplay just like I tell ya'. I mean you can use yer usual tricks and stuff. . . . Yer artistic hocus pocus. But ya gotta' write everything like I say. Every move. . . . You finish the whole thing up for me. Top to bottom. And you put my name on it. And I own all the rights. And every dime goes into my pocket. You do all that and I'll sure enough take ya' with me to the desert.[38]

Undeterred by Lee's exorbitant demands, Austin quickly agrees, and in Scene Nine the brothers begin their collaboration in earnest. Lee is clearly in control now, dictating both the pace and content of their creation. Like the prototypical philistine producer who has neither any respect for, nor any comprehension of, the artistic process, he demands that Austin be utterly obeisant and, at the same time, original. Austin does his best to comply, and in short order is turning out what can only be termed "hack work."

AUSTIN (reading) 'I told ya' you were a fool to follow me in here. I know this prairie like the back of my hand.'
LEE   No, no, No. That's not what I said. I never said that . . . that's stupid. That's one a' those—whatya call it? What d'ya call that? . . . A cliche.
AUSTIN That's what you said.
LEE   I never said that! And if I did, that's where yer supposed to come in. That's where yer supposed to change it to somethin' better.
         . . . .
AUSTIN Um—How 'bout—'I'm on intimate terms with this prairie.'
         . . . .
LEE   That's good. I like that. That's real good.
AUSTIN You do?
LEE   Yeah. Don't you?[39]

As this collaboration lurches on, Mom unexpectedly returns from her vacation. Having left her home in Austin's seemingly capable hands, she is shocked to find the place in such disarray.[40] By way of explanation, Austin tells her that they have been "celebratin" the sale of Lee's screenplay and that once finished, he "and Lee are going out to the desert to live."[41] Mom is astonished.

MOM   You and Lee?
AUSTIN Yeah. I'm taking off with Lee.
MOM   (She looks back and forth at each of them. Pause) You gonna live with your father?

AUSTIN   No. We're going to a different desert, Mom.
MOM   I see. Well, you'll probably wind up on the same desert sooner or later.⁴²

Mom recognizes that in her absence, the son with whom she has long been allied,⁴³ has suddenly fallen prey to his father's curse. She attempts to break the spell by reminding him that he "can't leave . . . [he has] a family."⁴⁴ Austin, nevertheless, remains adamant. Like Weston, the father in *Curse of the Starving Class*, and his own father and brother, he has come to perceive family life as a microcosm of society-at-large, and, as such, a form of incarceration from which one must flee, no matter the damage done those left behind. As Doris Auerbach points out,

> The sons [in Shepard's family plays] are unable to end the repetition of abandonment. They're doomed to repeat the obsessive behavior of the the fathers, rootless wanderers. . . . [who] leave wives and children in the elusive search for themselves.⁴⁵

For Austin, like so many of Shepard's men, true masculinity is defined in Darwinian terms, as something singular and solitary, where one's only task is to survive in a world seen as wholly adversarial.

Mom, however, doesn't see her younger son as being up to such a "task," maintaining that "he's too thin."⁴⁶ And Lee, who had been comparatively quiet up until that point, quickly concurs: "Yeah, he'd just burn up out there."⁴⁷ Utterly unaffected by the promise he had made Austin earlier, Lee has decided suddenly to abandon both his brother and the screenplay, ransack his mother's house for silverware and china, and go back to the desert alone.

Outraged at being betrayed by his brother a second time and, perhaps more significantly, at being denied access to his father and the life he represents, Austin reacts violently. Grabbing a telephone cord, he wraps it around Lee's neck and begins to strangle him. Having so attacked his brother, Austin has, in fact, trapped himself: if he loosens the cord, Lee will kill him, and if he doesn't, he will kill Lee, thereby destroying his only hope for a new life. In an attempt to extricate himself, he gets Lee to give up the car keys. This does not solve his problem, however. He cannot escape unless he lets go of the cord, and if Austin does, Lee will not let him escape. Hence, Austin desperately tries to convince himself that he is a true Darwinian male; capable of both killing rather than being killed and of going off into the wilderness alone. At this point, Mom, "powerless to intercede and stop the endless progression from one violent man to another,"[48] withdraws. Declaring her home—and one may also argue, her sons—to be unrecognizable, she decides to check into a motel. In response, Austin shows his true colors: rather than finish off his brother and take off into the desert, he pleads with his mother to stay, promising to "get everything fixed up."[49]

Mom leaves nonetheless, forcing Austin to make a deal reminiscent of the one made by the adulterous cowboy in Lee's story:

> You let me get outa' here. Just let me get to my car. All right, Lee? Gimme a little headstart and I'll turn you loose. Just gimme a little headstart. All right?[50]

Lee, playing possum, remains silent. As soon, however, as Austin makes a move to leave, Lee leaps up blocking his escape. With a confrontation imminent, Shepard abruptly shifts locales; moving from the particular and realistic to the more abstract and universal.

> [As the brothers] square off to each other, keeping a distance between them . . . a single coyote is heard . . . [The] lights fade softly to moonlight . . . [and] the figures of the brothers now appear to be caught in a vast desert-like landscape. They are very still but watchful for the next move.[51]

Certain critics view this, the play's final tableau, as representing the brothers' insoluable struggle. David DeRose sees Austin and Lee as "fighting on against the backdrop of eternity,"[52] while William Kleb, arguing that Lee and Austin are but warring aspects of a single divided self, states that the ending "leaves [their] basic condition unresolved."[53] It is my contention, however, that the play's final tableau signifies an imminent and forseeable resolution. By suddenly situating the two brothers in the desert, Shepard has brought us to the climactic moment of Lee's familial allegory where the pursued, having led his pursuer into a no-man's land that only he knows, suddenly turns and confronts his uncertain and ill-prepared opponent.[54] A final battle, much like those between Pop and Ice in *The Holy Ghostly* and Hoss and Crow in *The Tooth of Crime*, is about to take place and there is little doubt that, as in those plays, it shall be the more vicious and unscrupulous combatant (in this case, Lee) who shall prevail.

In the end, as the brothers square off in this most unequal contest, it becomes clear that *True West* is, in essence, a revenge drama in which the absent father, through a surrogate, punishes his younger son for having dared attempt to renounce him, for having succeeded in ways in which he himself was incapable.

Notes

1 Charles. R. Lyons, "Shepard's Family Trilogy and the Conventions of Modern Realism," *Rereading Shepard*, ed. Leonard Wilcox (New York: St. Martin's Press, 1993), 128.

2 *Sam Shepard* (New York: Continuum, 1992), 140.

3 Lynda Hart, *Sam Shepard's Metaphorical Stages* (Westport, Conn: Greenwood Press, 1987), 100.

4 Albeit not on quite the same scale as his father.

5 Sam Shepard, *True West* (Garden City, NY: Doubleday), 8.

6 Ibid., 6–7.

7 Ibid., 13.

8 It is Austin whom their mother entrusted to care for her home in her absence.

9 *True West*, 5.

10 Ibid.

11 Ibid., 11.

12 Ibid., 15.

13 Ibid., 16.

14 Ibid., 30–31.

15 Ibid., 21.

16 It should also be noted that in extricating himself from his father's grip, Austin either accompanied, followed, or was followed by his mother to California. It may therefore be argued that, like the pursued cowboy in Lee's story, Austin too has stolen the affections of the pursuer's wife.

17 It is ambiguous as to whether Lee in fact intends to parcel out money to his father or has simply used his father's plight as a way to further gain Kimmer's sympathy and is intent on keeping the money himself.

18 *True West*, 41–42.

19 Ibid., 42.

20 In Scene Seven, Austin describes a visit to the old man in which he offered him money "and all he did was play Al Jolson records and spit at me." *True West*, 52.

21 *True West*, 46.

22 This is the first time in the play that Austin is drunk, and marks but another step in his march towards his father.

23 *True West*, 48.

24 Ibid., 52.

25 Ibid., 53.

26 Ibid.

27 Ibid., 52.

28 Ibid., 55.

29 *Sam Shepard's Metaphorical Stages*, 93.

30 A number of critics view *True West* as chronicling, among other things, a love triangle. Sheila Rabillard argues that "one can . . . see the drama as structured about . . . two men's rivalry for the love of their father," while Martin Tucker states "the two brothers refer to the father several times and . . . are rivals for his approval/affection." Charles Lyons elaborates on this idea, contending that "*True West* exercises a structural convention that is a particularly American variant of dramatic realism: the opposition of two brothers caught in a triangular relationship with their father." See Rabillard, "Shepard's Challenge to the Modernist Myths of Origin and Originality: *Angel City* and *True West*," *Rereading Shepard*, ed. Leonard Wilcox (New York: St. Martin's Press, 1993), 86, Tucker, *Sam Shepard*, 139, and Lyons "Shepard's Family Trilogy and the Conventions of Modern Realism," 128.

31 *True West*, 61.

32 Ibid., 62.

33 It needs to be noted that Austin is but one more of Shepard's fleeing fathers, and is prepared to abandon his wife and children as readily as did both his own father and Weston, the father in *Curse of The Starving Class*.

34 *True West*, 63.

35 Ibid., 64.

36 It is significant that in Shepard's family plays (i.e., *Curse of the Starving Class* and *Buried Child*), it is only by falling prey to the father's curse that such authenticity is achieved.

37 *True West*, 64.

38 Ibid., 64–65.

39 Ibid., 67–68.

40　In fact, what her sons have done is to recreate their father's home in hers. (Shepard describes it as looking "like a desert junkyard at high noon." *True West*, 66).

41　Ibid., 70.

42　Ibid.

43　William Kleb points out quite accurately that at the play's beginning, Austin's identification with his mother is as obvious as Lee's with "the old man." See "Worse Than Being Homeless: *True West* and the Divided Self," *American Dreams: The Imagination of Sam Shepard*, ed. Bonnie\ Marranca (New York: Performing Arts Journal Publications, 1981), 119.

44　*True West*, 72.

45　"Who Was Icarus's Mother? The Powerless Mother Figures in the Plays of Sam Shepard," *Sam Shepard: A Casebook*, (New York: Garland, 1988), 54–55.

46　*True West*, 72.

47　Ibid.

48　Auerbach, "Who Was Icarus's Mother?," 54.

49　*True West*, 72.

50　Ibid., 77.

51　Ibid.

52　"A Kind of Cavorting: Superpresence and Shepard's Family Dramas," *Rereading Shepard*, ed. Leonard Wilcox (New York: St. Martin's Press, 1993), 143.

53　"Worse Than Being Homeless," 100.

54　It is clear that while Lee was initially his brother's pursuer, he has by the play's end become—in keeping with his story—the pursued, the betrayer who lures his brother onto a prairie with which he "is on intimate terms"—that is, one of violence and retribution—in order to destroy him.

Chapter Seven

A Lie of the Mind: The Curse's End

To anyone familiar with the Shepard canon it is clear that in *A Lie of the Mind*, he is, in certain respects, mining territory he has mined before.[1] It should be pointed out, however, that while *A Lie of the Mind* is indeed a conspicuous amalgam of themes, structures, character-types, and objects utilized in the plays we have already analyzed, it is nevertheless a work which stands firmly apart from those plays. Far from being a somewhat imaginative rehash of earlier work, *A Lie of the Mind* is in many ways a refutation of the themes and ideas Shepard had previously espoused. Here he has created a world where the past is not the future and where biology is not ultimately one's destiny. Furthermore, *A Lie of the Mind* is a comparatively optimistic work where "the survival of the fittest" is no longer defined in terms of amorality and a capacity for violence,[2] but by emotional generosity, contrition, and the eventual acceptance of long-denied truths.

The play begins on familiar ground,[3] with a "cursed" protagonist, Jake, calling his younger brother Frankie from a pay phone on the highway. He has beaten up a woman (yet unnamed), so badly in fact that he believes he has killed her. Distraught and perplexed, Jake cannot understand why he is suddenly compelled to commit such acts:[4]

> I never even see it comin'. I shoulda known. Why didn't I see it comin'. I been good for so long. . . . She's not gonna pull outa this one, Frankie. . . . It was bad this time. Real bad . . . [and] I never even saw it comin', Frankie. I never did. How come that is? How come?[5]

Much like Weston and Wesley in *Curse of the Starving Class*, Jake is prone to fits of violence which come upon him intermittently and without warning, and which he naively thinks he can control ("I been good for so long"). One thing which distinguishes this scene, and by extension this drama, from Shepard's earlier father-son plays is that Jake reaches out to his brother in his moment of crisis. In marked contrast to Shepard's other siblings (Tilden and Bradley, in *Buried Child*, and Lee and Austin in *True West*), Jake and Frankie are not enemies locked in some interminable competition for their parents' affections. Rather, they are allies, with the younger brother serving as his middle-aged brother's almost paternal caretaker.

In the first act's second scene, we discover that the woman beaten is Jake's wife, Beth, and that she is not dying. She has, however, been deeply traumatized and her speech vacillates wildly. At times it is utter blather, while at other times she speaks a fractured but comprehensible type of poetry; at still other moments she is completely coherent. Attended to by her brother, Mike, she begins the scene by ripping off the bandages wrapped around her head, demanding that

> You tell them, I'm not dead. You go tell them. Tell them now. Go tell them. Dig me up. Tell them dig me up now. I'm not in here. . . . Iza toomb. Iza toomb! You tell them I'm not dead.[6]

It is not clear at this point which "them" Beth is referring to—her own family, Jake and his, or the hospital staff. What is apparent, however, is that Beth, despite the damage done her, is intent on being recognized as still living (in the fullest sense), as having an autonomous identity, and as such still capable of exercising free will.[7] Having been raised, as we learn later, in a household where her "crazy" grandmother was brought and kept, she accuses Mike of being the family's lackey sent to abduct her.

> They leave you here to bring me back? Did they leave you. . . . Yore the dog. Yore the dog they send. . . . [but] You gant take in me. You gant take me back.[8]

Unlike Ella and Emma in *Curse of the Starving Class* and Halie in *Buried Child*, who fail in their attempts to create lives for themselves outside the family, Beth has been able, in some measure, to break free.[9] And it is free she wishes to remain. For Beth, home represents not a sanctuary but a prison, a place where only the warden's needs are met, and the wife and children are sentenced to lives of utter servitude ("Yore the dog they send").

In the first act's third scene, we return to Jake and Frankie, who are now in some ragged highway motel.[10] Having regained command of himself, Jake declares it was those "damn rehearsals"[11] that Beth was "goin' to . . . very day"[12] and the way she prepared for them that set him off.

> I'm no dummy. Doesn't take much to put it together. Woman starts dressin' more and more skimpy. Starts puttin' on more and more smells. . . . I'd watch her oiling herself. . . . She was in a dream, the way she did it. Like she was imagining someone else touching her. Not me. Never me. Someone else. . . . Some actor-jerk.[13]

As Jake continues his "defense," he concedes that while Beth was not in fact literally unfaithful, she was nonetheless guilty on some subliminal level.

> JAKE   . . . . I knew what she was up to even if she didn't.
> FRANKIE   So, you mean you're accusing her of somethin' she wasn't even aware of?[14]

We discover by the end of Jake's account that Beth's only "crime" was to have discovered, so to speak, "a room of her own." Interpreting Beth's newfound vocation as the means "to get away from me,"[15] thereby confirming his overwhelming sense of unworthiness, Jake retaliates as he has always retaliated: with extreme violence.

Now, however, Jake is desperate to avoid responsibility for what he has done. If he is to survive, Beth, somehow, must be shown to be at fault. Frankie, however, refuses to accept Jake's version of things. He points out that Jake has always had a bad temper, and that throughout his life he has always sought to blame those he had physically hurt. In the face of this truth and the guilt it calls forth, Jake suddenly collapses. The snarling, rageful character we observed at the beginning of the scene, having been denied one of his life-sustaining lies, has suddenly been reduced to a weak, whispering ghost. In what is his first display of remorse, he confesses to Frankie that:

> I'm gonna die without her. I know I'm gonna die. . . . This fear, it swarms through me—floods my whole body till there's nothing left. Nothing left of me. And then it turns—it turns to fear for my whole life. Like my whole life is lost from losing her.[16]

By the fourth scene, Beth's condition has improved. She is now not only able to walk but to more clearly articulate her concerns, which at this point center on Jake. She pleads with Mike not to hurt her husband, explaining that he (Jake) is "a chile."[17] Beth recognizes both Jake's vulnerability and his inability to control himself. Furthermore, as Ron Mottram and Janet Haedicke point out, she is prescient enough to know the degree to which Jake is now suffering,[18] and that in trying to destroy her, he has destroyed himself as well. Mike, however, is neither interested in Jake's frailties nor the extent of his suffering. To him, Jake is simply a murderer. He commands his sister not to "THINK ABOUT HIM!"[19]—to in fact "just forget about him."[20] In response, Beth angrily declares that she (unlike her husband) "IS NOT A BABY!"[21] and goes on to assert that

> you gan' stop my head. Nobody! Nobody stop my head. My head is me. Heez in me. You gan stop him in me. Nobody can stop him in me.[22]

It is via this speech that Shepard reveals one "lie of the mind," the belief that one, through insistent bullying, can control the thoughts and feelings—and therefore the actions—of another.

Act One, Scene Five begins with a tableau almost identical to that which opens *Buried Child*: a man, his face obscured, lies motionless on a couch, covered by a blanket. To assume, however, that Shepard views Jake, the wife-beater, as but a younger version of Dodge, the child-murderer, would be to discount the significant differences existing between the two. While both men are criminals, and harbor secrets which eventually become the dramatic focal points of their respective plays (more on this later), the manner in which they respond to their crimes places them in almost diametric opposition. Whereas Jake lies on his couch immobilized with guilt at having harmed the person he treasures most, Dodge hides himself away on his merely 1) to escape his family, most notably his wife, and 2) because he is too old and weak to do anything else. In fact, Dodge is utterly without remorse. In a speech to Shelly he reveals that his was an act motivated by practicality, a way in which to hide a still earlier crime which, if discovered, would have savaged his family's reputation. Hence, regardless of what we think of Jake, we must acknowledge that he, at least, is not without conscience.

As the scene proceeds, Jake is visited by his mother, Lorraine, and his sister, Sally. Much like her comatose son, Lorraine is quick to disavow any personal responsibility for what Jake has done.

> He was trouble from day one. Fell on his damn head the second he was born. . . . That's where it all started. Back there. *Had nothin' to do with his upbringing.* (emphasis mine)[23]

Having excused herself, Lorraine goes on to absolve Jake as well, redefining him as an amoral innocent, a mere force of nature, and again like her son, places the blame on Beth, the victim, a woman she claims she never heard of.[24]

> He wasn't fit to live with anybody to begin with! I don't know why he ever tried it. Woman who lives with a man like that deserves to be killed. She deserves it.[25]

Furthermore, unable to accept the severity of Jake's condition, or its cause, she declares it is "just play-acting. Used to do this all the time when he didn't get his own way."[26] Much like Halie in *Buried Child*, another mother riddled with "lies of the mind," Lorraine lives, in large measure, in a world of her own invention, fending off the more unacceptable realities with blame and misinterpretation. Unlike Halie, however, who despite her actions maintains a genteel facade, Lorraine, much like her son, is given to fits of violence. Hence when Jake grabs hold of Sally, mistaking her for Beth, Lorraine quickly jumps in, first beating Jake with a shoe, and then beating Frankie when he attempts to break things up.[27]

Finally, Lorraine decides that the only solution to Jake's problems is to bring him home "on a permanent basis."[28] At this, Sally balks. She doesn't want to live in the same house as her "crazy" and "dangerous" brother. Lorraine, however, roughly brushes aside her daughter's objections. Intent on reclaiming her son (for reasons which will become clear later), she coldly tells Sally "then leave, girl. This is my boy here."[29]

Having introduced the living members of Jake's family in the preceding scene, Shepard maintains the play's symmetrical structure by introducing, in Scene Six, Beth's parents, both of whom, while having certain attributes common to Shepard's earlier mothers and fathers, are nonetheless unique creations. Unlike Weston in *Curse of the Starving Class*, "the old man" in *True West*, or for that matter, Jake's father (who has yet to be introduced), Baylor has neither abandoned his family nor is he a drunkard. That said, it should be pointed out that Baylor is certainly as imperiously contentious and nearly as self-absorbed as any of the fathers (and father surrogates) we've previously analyzed. Having driven down from Montana, ostensibly to see his daughter, he soon reveals his true motives lay elsewhere:

> BAYLOR Wake her up. We drove all the way down here from Billings just to see her. Now wake her up.

MIKE	She's having a rough time right now, Dad. She needs a lot of rest.
BAYLOR	Listen, I got two mules settin' out there in the parkin' lot I gotta deliver by midnight. I'm supposed to be at the sale by six tommorrow mornin' and those mules have to be in the stalls by midnight tonight.
MIKE	You brought mules down here?
BAYLOR	Yeah. Why not? Might as well do a little business long as I'm gonna be down in this country anyway. That all right by you?[30]

Baylor is, in fact, obsessed with his own well-being. Consequently, when his wife Meg decides to stay with Beth a few days before accompanying her brain-damaged daughter back to their home, Baylor demands to know "What am *I* supposed to do, talk to myself all the way back home? That's a five hundred mile truck trip."[31]

In the end, however, Baylor does defer to Meg's wishes, and in so doing, reveals that he is not altogether lacking in compassion.

BAYLOR	You wanna stay?
MEG	I'd like to.
BAYLOR	Alright. (*To* MIKE) How many days you think it'll be?
MIKE	Two or three.
MEG	I'll be fine, Baylor.
BAYLOR	You'll be fine. You'll be fine. Sure. All right. I'll go out and get your jacket out of the truck. Be right back.
MEG	I won't need it.
BAYLOR	(*As he exits*) You'll need it. You always need it. (BAYLOR *exits.* MEG *turns and smiles at* MIKE)
MEG	He's right.[32]

As this exchange indicates, Baylor views Meg essentially as a child, a view which the scene as a whole seems to support. At first, Meg appears to be but a kinder and decidedly more comic version of O'Neill's Mary Tyrone:[33] confused, forgetful,[34] and prone to unprovoked reveries. As the play progresses, however, this initial interpretation of Meg gives way to its antithesis, and we eventually come to look upon her as a woman of extraordinary strength, virtue, and wisdom.[35]

In Act One, Scene Seven we find Lorraine and Jake alone together onstage, just as we had Ella and Wesley at the conclusion of *Curse of the Starving Class*. In fact, with the sister gone (albeit, in this case, still living), the father dead, and the curse-riddled son now middle-aged, one feels, initially at least, as if one is revisiting the Tates after a twenty year absence. Shepard drives home this analogy by placing the scene's action in Jake's bedroom, a room whose most notable feature, like that of Wesley's in *Curse of the Starving Class*, is a collection of "plastic model airplanes [now] covered in dust and cobwebs of World War Two fighters and bombers [which] hang from the ceiling directly above the bed."[36]

As the scene unfolds, it also calls forth comparisons to both *Buried Child* and *True West*. While spoonfeeding her son, Lorraine describes Jake as a "strong, strappin man. . .[with] a big stout frame,"[37] just like his drunkard father, a man who even "at the age of sixty . . . still managed to twirl my ticket."[38] Here, as in *Buried Child*, there is the intimation of incestuous attraction which, while never realized, certainly suggests that Lorraine's interest in her son is not purely maternal. Having been abandoned by her husband years before,[39] Lorraine attempts to rectify the past by recreating it, with her son serving as the emotional, if not physical, husband-surrogate who will forever stand by her. Jake, however, has other plans. Upon learning that Frankie has gone off to see Beth, he decides, in spite of his weakened condition, to make his way to Montana—a decision Lorraine adamantly opposes. Not about to be abandoned again, to have the past reassert itself once more at her expense, she tells Jake that he's "not going anywhere,"[40] that he "never should a' left [here] in the first place,"[41] and as part of a ludicrous strategy to detain her son, hides his pants.

As their conversation continues, Jake asks to see the box containing his father's ashes, which as it turns out is underneath his bed.[42] He then questions Lorraine as to the circumstances surrounding his father's death.

JAKE   How was it he died?
              (*Pause. They stare at each other*)
LORRAINE   Jake, you remember all that.
JAKE   No, I don't remember. I don't remember it at all.
              . . . .
LORRAINE   He burned up.
JAKE   His plane crashed?
LORRAINE   No . . . Got hit by a truck. Drunk as a snake out in the middle of the highway. Truck blew up and he went with it. You already know that.
              (JAKE *leaps to his feet but stays by the bed.*)
JAKE   DON'T TELL ME I ALREADY KNOW SOMETHIN' I DON'T KNOW! DON'T TELL ME THAT! HOW COULD I KNOW SOMETHIN' THAT I DON'T KNOW?
              . . . .

> LORRAINE (*Quietly*) Because you were there, Jake. You were right there with him when it happened.[43]

Suddenly, as in *Buried Child*, we find ourselves in the middle of a mystery dealing with the death of a family member. Whereas previously the play's central dramatic question was whether Jake and Beth would reconcile, Shepard now poses a second dramatic question: What part did Jake play in his father's death?

Near the end of Act One, Shepard has shifted the play's focus from what *might* happen to what *has* happened, from the future to the past, and in the concluding moments of the first act, shows Jake redirecting his attention away from Beth and towards his father.

> JAKE [*stares*] *out across to stage left. . . . Light begins to come up on* BETH's *hospital bed, now made up with blue satin sheets. . . . She is uninjured now—no bandage, her hair soft and beautiful. She is oiling her shoulders and chest . . . unaware of* JAKE. *She is simply his vision. Suddenly* JAKE *makes a move toward her and the lights on her black out. She disappears. . . . All the rest of the lights black out except for a tight spotlight on his father's box of ashes. . . .* [JAKE] *blows lightly into the box, sending a soft puff of ashes up into the beam of spotlight.*[44]

The implications of this sequence are fairly obvious. Not only is the Beth Jake hopes to reclaim unreachable, she no longer exists. She is but "a vision," a "lie of the mind" that cannot be sustained. For Jake, redemption now lies in the acknowledgement of his past misdeeds, in what he has done to both his father and wife.

Act Two begins with Beth now back home, overhearing an argument outside between Mike and a man whom she recognizes as having "Jake's . . . voice."[45] Mike, however, claims that the man is not Jake, and in fact, "got nothin to do with Jake. [He's] just some guy,"[46] but Beth doesn't believe him. Whether or not a consequence of her brain-damage, Beth is now able to see into the hearts and minds of others. She declares Mike a liar, the one who is truly "dead," and then, in a speech which sheds further light on the play's title, describes lying's insidious effects:

> You make—you make a war. You make a war. You make an enemy. In me. In me! An enemy. You. You. You think me. You think you know. You think. You have a big idea.[47]

Beth sees lying as a violence, an act dividing one individual from the next and in essence turning them into adversaries. By extension then, "a lie of the mind" denotes an internal war, one which turns the self into two warring halves; one which on some level knows the truth and one which denies it—the result being a type of madness which poisons the individual compelling it to behave in strange, and sometimes, terrible ways. As Meg succinctly puts it, try as it may, "the brain can't hide."[48]

In the face of Beth's diatribe, Mike admits that the man he confronted was Frankie, Jake's brother and that he is now gone. But, as it turns out, Frankie is not gone. Shot in the leg by Baylor, who mistook him for a deer, he is brought into the house to recuperate. Outraged by this sudden turn of events, Mike, as is typical of the play's "liars," blames the victim for the damage done him, telling Frankie:

> You wormed your way in, didn't you. Pretty cute. But I'm not forgettin' anything. Everybody else might forget but I'm not. Far as I'm concerned you and your brother are the same person.[49]

Mike then attempts to get Frankie out of the house, but when rebuffed by both Beth and Baylor,[50] is forced ironically, to leave home himself and move to the family's hunting shed. Possessed, as Jane Anne Crum states, by a "rigidity . . . [an] inability to forget, and by extension, to forgive,"[51] Mike appears to be an older, more wrathful incarnation of Wesley at the beginning of *Curse of the Starving Class*. Like his teenaged counterpart, Mike is intent on maintaining the family, on defending it against interlopers and attackers, even as the rest of the family prepares to disperse. With Baylor spending longer and longer periods alone in his hunting shed, and Beth and Meg moving towards greater self-sufficiency, Mike has taken it upon himself to serve (and, ideally, be recognized) as the family's champion, the man who, by example, can force his family to be as they once were.

At the scene's end, Beth finally addresses Frankie directly, revealing what Felicia Londre terms "a barometric sensitivity to others' capacity for love."[52] Having earlier defined her mother, Meg, as "a love. . . . Only that. Only. . . . Only love. Good. . . . Always love. Always,"[53] she describes her father to Frankie conversely as:

> [having] given up love. Love is dead for him. My mother is dead for him. Things live for him to be killed. Only death counts. Nothing else.[54]

Having looked deeply into the hearts of her parents and revealed what she has seen, Beth then turns her gaze upon herself, and subsequently upon Frankie:

> ([Moving] slowly towards FRANKIE) This is me. This is me now. The way I am. This. All. Different. I-I live inside this. Remember. Remembering. You. You—were one. I know you. I know—love. I know what love is. I can never forget that. Never.[55]

Beth clearly recognizes herself as irretrievably changed, as altogether new person. What is more ambiguous, however, is her confession of love. Is she admitting that Frankie was always the "one" she loved, or has she confused him with Jake? Or rather, is she declaring that with her new perceptional powers she can now see Frankie, like Meg, as a uniquely loving presence in a house—and by extension, a world—where men, as Lynda Hart notes, typically mistake pride or violent passion for love[56] ("I know you. I know—love.")?

Act Two, Scene Two begins with Jake shaving, while wearing but his underwear and "the old man's" bomber jacket. This initial image further reveals Jake to be a child in a man's body,[57] an underdeveloped individual much like Tilden in *Buried Child*, who despite his age has yet to achieve adulthood. Jake himself confirms as much when he confides to Sally (who has returned) the solution to his problems.

> I'll tell ya the only idea that's gonna work. . . . I'm not goin' outdoors anymore. I'm not leavin' this room. Mom brings me food. I don't need the outside. All I do is get in trouble out there.[58]

It is apparent from his "solution" that Jake has made little psychospiritual progress. Rather than accept responsibility for what he has done, he refutes the notion of responsibility altogether, choosing instead to blame "the outside" and be cared for like a child. Jake has decided that it is the world which is "crazy" and not him, and that it is both safer and saner to check himself back into the ward to which he was born, where, alone with his mother, he never need confront the truth.

Sally, however, refuses to accept his "solution." She tells him that "pretending to be crazy . . . [is] not gonna change what you did,"[59] thereby refocussing our attention upon the play's central mystery, their father's death. Furthermore, it is now apparent that not only does Sally know what happened "out there" in the desert but, as revealed in the ensuing exchange, Jake does too.

> JAKE   Sally—
> SALLY Don't worry. I'm not gonna give you away.
> JAKE   We made a promise.
> SALLY Yeah.
> JAKE   Don't forget.[60]

No sooner does Jake concede, however obliquely, that he did something "out there" that no one dare know about, then he immediately reasserts that he doesn't remember what that something is. He further attempts to redirect attention away from himself and the night his father died by desperately proclaiming that Lorraine and Frankie "got a pact.... They wanna make me suffer. Don't you know that? Frankie thinks I deserve to suffer. So does Mom."[61] Here again, we see Jake's behavioral modus operandi. Whenever he senses the truth closing in, whenever he experiences the slightest modicum of guilt, he immediately counters by presenting a situation where he is the innocent, the victim and not the victimizer.

Sally refutes this claim as well, stating quite accurately that "nobody wants to make you suffer. Only you."[62] She views her brother's paranoia as a species of self-contempt which he attempts to escape by projecting it onto others. It is at this moment that Lorraine appears. Unhappy at her daughter's return, she castigates Sally for her lack of initiative, for living a life where "everything just keeps repeatin' itself,"[63] and demands that she go.

> Why can't you just leave! Why can't you just get your fanny out in the wide world and find yourself somethin' to do. Stop mopin' around here gettin' everybody's dander up.[64]

Lorraine attacks her daughter for doing exactly what she herself has done. Despite her abandonment, Lorraine too has never ventured forth, preferring to stay put and wallow in her misfortune.

It is clear, however, that it is Sally's mere presence, and not her lack of initiative, which enrages Lorraine. Wanting her son for herself, wanting to recreate the life she once led with her husband, no matter how pitifully aberrant the recreation, Lorraine knows she cannot realize her plans if Sally remains. Hoping to have her demands seconded, she turns to Jake.

> Jake, look—we were doin' just fine, weren't we? We had everything workin' smooth as butter here. We had our system. We were self-sufficient, weren't we, Jake. What do we need her for?[65]

Jake, however, spurns his mother, deeming her plans for him "a trap."[66] He doesn't want Sally to leave. Spurred by her return, Jake suddenly appears ready to confront the events leading to his father's death, and his role in them.

JAKE Where was that, Sally. Where was that? Were we there when it happened?
SALLY You don't wanna know.
JAKE We drove all night long.
SALLY Just forget about it now.[67]

And "forget about it" he does, at least momentarily, for Shepard suddenly dispenses with the third wall and allows Jake to observe what is happening at that moment in Montana. Watching his wife attend to his wounded brother, Jake now knows that Beth is indeed alive and is seized instantly by the need to get to her.

Act Two, Scene Three is a continuation of what Jake had observed moments earlier. In the interim, Beth has taken off her shirt and is attempting to wrap it around Frankie's wound. Deeply unnerved by both the intensity of his sister-in-law's attention and her semi-nakedness, Frankie pleads with her repeatedly to put her shirt back on. Finally, Beth does take back the shirt, stating that "Jake was scared of shirts . . . too."[68] Whatever her previous confusions, it is apparent now that Beth views Frankie and Jake as separate individuals. Moreover, she can discern (and is attracted to) a gentleness in Frankie which Jake never possessed. Asking him to act like Jake "but soft. With me. . . . Like a woman-man,"[69] Beth sees her brother-in-law neither as Jake nor a Jake surrogate, but as a distinct individual whom, in fact, she could fully love.

> You could be better [than Jake]. Better man. Maybe. Without hate. You could be my sweet man. You could . . . Try. My sweetest man. . . . You could really fall in love with me. How would that be? In a love we never knew.[70]

Beth recognizes that it is "the woman-man . . . . [the man] without hate" who is capable of true love. Here we see Shepard expanding upon an idea he first put forth in *The Tooth of Crime*. Having defined the young Gypsy, Crow, as the incarnation of pure evil because he deliberately killed the feminine part of himself, Shepard now goes on to define the good self as that in which the masculine and feminine coexist.[71]

Frankie, ever loyal to his brother, resists Beth's overtures, and when Mike returns (depositing a deer carcass on the living room floor), he pleads with him to "get me outa here anyway you can."[72] Mike, however, senses Frankie's desperation and refuses. Intent on punishing Jake's younger brother by whatever means available, he merely smiles and exits. Frankie, exhausted, then collapses on the couch, and for the first time, allows Beth to console him.

> (Patting him softly on his head) Your whole life can turn around. Upside down. In a flash. Sudden. Don't worry. Don't worry now. This whole world can disappear.[73]

Here, Shepard explicitly states the play's major theme—one which differs radically from those of *The Tooth of Crime*, *Curse of the Starving Class*, and *Buried Child*. Having herself experienced what David J. DeRose terms "a perceptual rebirth,"[74] Beth realizes that change is possible, that the self, despite the damage done it, can recreate itself in new and better ways, and that the world to which it has long been subjected—one the play has hitherto characterized as violent, self-interested, self-deceiving, and subservient to the past—can "in a flash . . . disappear."[75]

In Act Two, Scene Four, Jake, with Sally's help, prepares to make his escape. Dressed still in only his underwear, the bomber jacket, and having added his father's flag (which he wears like a cape), he looks like a little boy running away from home. Yet it is apparent from his speech at the scene's end that Jake is not the man-child he once was but, like his wife, has begun to change:

> There's this thing—this thing in my head. . . . a voice. A scream from a voice I don't know. Or a voice I knew once but now it's changed. It doesn't know me either. Now. It used to but not now. I've scared it into something else. Another form. A whole other person who doesn't see me anymore. Who doesn't even remember that we knew each other. I've gotta see her again, Sally.[76]

At long last, Jake has begun to assume responsibility for what he has done. He admits to having "scared [Beth] into . . . a whole other person who doesn't . . . even remember that we knew each other,"[77] without concomitantly attempting to lay the blame elsewhere.

Act Three begins with Lorraine in her son's bed, sick and suffering with chills. Having been abandoned by Jake just as she was by his father, having been defeated in her battle to amend the past, Lorraine has collapsed.[78] She is still, however, a "strong" enough "liar" to blame Sally for her present misfortune, accusing her daughter of having "put [Jake] up to it."[79] Furthermore, as the scene progresses, Lorraine attempts to render Sally still guiltier by describing in apocalyptic terms what will happen to Jake now that Sally has freed him:

> Now he's gonna wind up right back in prison. . . . . [Either that or] they'll find him by the highway. That's what'll happen. Crumbled up. Busted open like a road dog. Then maybe you'll be satisfied.[80]

Fed up with her mother's accusations and her view of herself and Jake as innocents at the mercy of a malevolent world, Sally decides to tell Lorraine how her husband died:[81]

> [We were] in his trailer . . . when [Jake] offers to take Dad and me out to a bar. . . . They started right off with double shots of tequila. At first it was like this brotherhood . . . [but] after about he fourth double shot. . . . there was this meanness that started to come outa both of them like these hidden snakes. A terrible meanness that was like—murder. It was murder.[82]

Drunk and bloodthirsty, Jake challenges his father to a foot race, one which he knows that "the old man" will not refuse and cannot win.

> He [Dad] crouched down in a racing position right beside Jake. . . . And then they took off. Dad took four strides and fell flat on his face . . . but Jake never stopped. He ran . . . straight into the next bar. . . . [Dad] wouldn't let me help him up. He just crawled . . . toward the bar that Jake went into. . . . [Then] Jake came up with a brilliant idea. He said since we were only about a mile from the American border we should hit every bar and continue the race . . . . First one to the other side won. . . . Right then I knew what Jake had in mind. . . . Jake had decided to kill him.[83]

And in the end, Jake succeeds. Goading his father on, Jake, much like the adulterous cowboy in Lee's story in *True West*, leads "the old man" to a place where he is lost, confused, and unable to defend himself.

> Dad couldn't even walk anymore. He couldn't stand. . . . didn't even know what country he was in . . . [and then] I saw it happen. I saw him splattered all over the road like some lost piece of livestock. . . . Jake murdered him! And he never looked back. He was already sitting in some bar. . . . never even got up when he heard the sirens.[84]

Here, for the first time in our analysis of Shepard's father-son plays, we see a son who both premeditatedly sets out to destroy his father and succeeds. Unlike in the earlier plays, where the fathers died either symbolically, by their own hands, or of natural causes,[85] in *A Lie of the Mind*, the accursed father is consciously destroyed by the son he has infected, by his younger, stronger double.

Having listened to her daughter's account, Lorraine, true to form, declares it "claptrap," going so far as to deem Sally the true murderer.

> LORRAINE . . . You stood there and watched your own father get run over by a truck in the middle of a Mexican highway and you're tryin' to tell me that Jake murdered him.

SALLY	That's the way it happened.
LORRAINE	What about you? Jake was nowhere near him you said. What were you doin'? Standing there helpless. You were the only one sober and there was nothin' you could do? Is that the story?[86]

Somehow, however, the truth of Sally's story strikes a chord long hidden in Lorraine, and although she never retracts her accusation, she too appears to have changed. Having been presented with a picture of just how deeply lost her husband was, and her son is, she's finally ready to break free. Her first act is to get rid of all of Jake's and his father's "junk."

> All these airplanes are comin' down. . . . All the junk in this house that they left behind for me to save. It's all goin'. . . . They had no intention of ever comin' back here to pick it up. That was just a dream of theirs . . . just to keep me on the hook. Can't believe I fell for it all those years.[87]

Lorraine now realizes that the men in her life, these runaways whose return she had long awaited, were always "hopeless" and that there's "nothin you can do about the hopeless."[88] Sick at the beginning of the scene, Lorraine has regained her strength.[89] She has, metaphorically speaking, sweated out the "lie" which infected her these many years, and is prepared finally to forge a new life.

In Act Three, Scene Two, we see Meg experiencing an awakening similar to that of Lorraine's in the preceding scene. Throughout the play, we have seen Meg essentially as Baylor sees her, a confused woman quick to acquiesce to her husband's needs. Now, suddenly, Meg rebels, and by doing so reveals herself in a new light. As she attends to her husband's badly blistered feet, she accuses Baylor of falsely thinking himself the family's martyr.

MEG	You think it's me, don't you?. . . . You think your whole life went sour because of me. Because of Mother. Because of Beth. If only your life was free of females, then you'd be freed yourself.
BAYLOR	Well, you sure know how to speak the truth when you put your mind to it, don't ya?
MEG	All these women put a curse on you and now you're stuck. You're chained to us forever. Isn't that the way it is?
BAYLOR	Yeah! Yeah! that exactly the way it is. . . . I gotta play nursemaid to a bunch a' feebleminded women down here in civilization who can't take care of themselves. I gotta waste my days away makin' sure they eat and have a roof over their heads and a nice warm place to go crazy in.[90]

Meg then asserts her autonomy even more radically. Pulling away from her husband, she declares that it is Baylor's perceptions and not hers which are askew, that she can and has always been able to look after herself, and that rather than continue to "suffer" at the hands of this menagerie of "madwomen," he should leave.

> Nobody's crazy, Baylor. Except you. Why don't you just go. Why don't you just go off and live the way you want to live. We'll take care of ourselves. We always have.[91]

As this speech indicates (most notably, in its last two lines) Meg has long known what Lorraine has only recently discovered: that the men they've attempted to please are not indispensible, and they can, in fact, survive without them. Furthermore, this speech forces us to look at Meg's past behavior from a new perspective. Contrary to what had earlier seemed to be the case, Meg's decision to serve as her husband's caretaker is motivated by neither a sense of powerlessness nor a fear of abandonment. Rather, it is a conscious choice. Unlike her "crazy" husband, whose madness is, in effect, the inability to transcend the self and its demands, Meg understands that it is only through generosity, through the free offer of oneself to another, that true love is manifested. As Jane Ann Crum observes,

> Generosity, the most unique and superlative quality of the feminine . . . would seem to be the basis of Meg's . . . revolution in *A Lie of the Mind*, a solution entirely opposite to Lorraine and Sally's choice to flee the fatherland, and as mysterious and subtle as theirs is conscious and verbalized.[92]

Having, in essence, declared her independence, Meg leaves Baylor to attend to himself and goes upstairs to Beth. Unable even to put on his own socks, Baylor curses his own body for "bein' so tied up in knots you can't even stand up to your wife."[93] Then, in an attempt to re-establish his dominance and by extension, his manhood,[94] he attacks the sleeping Frankie, first by declaring him a "goddamn freeloader"[95] and then by demanding that Frankie, despite his wounds, help him with his socks.

Driven to exasperation by Baylor and his children, Frankie demands to know why "nobody around here will try and make any effort to get me outa here."[96] Warning Baylor of his brother's "short fuse," he goes on to confess that his sister-in-law has been behaving in ways that would "tip [Jake] over the edge."[97]

> Your daughter. She is getting very strange with me. Very strange. I mean she started talkin' to me like I was him. Like I was my brother. To her, I mean. Like she thought I was him and not me. Your daughter, Beth.[98]

It is clear from this speech that Frankie, although loyal, altruistic, and in many instances a truth-teller, is not without his own "lie of the mind." Unable to accept that Beth's feelings for him are genuine, or that he himself may harbor similar feelings,[99] he willfully misrepresents Beth as "strange" and confused.

It is at this point that Meg and Beth reappear to refute Frankie's "lie." Beth has decided to marry Frankie whom she sees clearly as a man worthy of her heart and not merely a pale incarnation of his brother.[100] Characterized by David J. DeRose as a woman who has "recreated herself, her world . . . without the enforced preconceptions of experience,"[101] Beth has no interest in either resurrecting her past or, as Susan Bennett points out, assuming "the wife/mother roles [of Meg] or Lorraine."[102] Rather, she wishes to move away from Jake and the madness of their relationship, and towards one fraught with real promise. Frankie, however, continues to resist, maintaining, "I AM NOT GETTIN' MARRIED TO MY BROTHER'S WIFE."[103]

It is then that Mike triumphantly enters, declaring that he has captured Jake and tied him to the cabin stove. Driven by the need for retribution, Mike has subjugated his enemy and subjected him to a series of humiliations which he proudly wishes to share with his family. As if in response to Mike's proclamation and the violent male ethos it represents, Beth consoles Frankie, reassuring him that "it's all right. Once we're together, the whole world will change. You'll see. We'll be in a whole new world."[104]

In Act Three, Scene Three, we return to Lorraine and Sally who, true to their word, are busy cleaning house,[105] divesting themselves of all memorabilia associated with Jake and his father. Having tossed the smaller items into a metal bucket, Sally asks her mother what they're going to do with the larger stuff. In response, Lorraine proposes an even more extreme act of emancipation.

> LORRAINE [Well] We're not gonna haul it. We're gonna burn it.
> SALLY I know, but we've gotta get it outa the house somehow.
> LORRAINE What for?
> SALLY Well, what're we gonna do, burn the house down?
> LORRAINE Why not?
>
> . . . .

SALLY   Well, we're not gonna have any place to come back to, Mom.
LORRAINE   Who's comin back?[106]

The symbolic significance of these proposed conflagrations is obvious. Lorraine is determined to create a new life for herself and her daughter, a life which will begin with a journey to Ireland.[107] Having, with Sally's help, abandoned her false hopes, Lorraine now perceives existence as an open-ended adventure, where the past is not the future, and where free will can flourish.

Finally, with her daughter watching and their bags packed, Lorraine strikes a match and tosses it into the bucket, thereby unsealing their fates once and for all. The lights then simultaneously dim on mother and daughter and come up on Jake, who, like his wife at the beginning of the play, is now bruised and black-eyed. Walking on his bloodied hands and knees (much like his dying father), "the American flag between his teeth and stretched taut on either side like a set of . . . reins,"[108] Jake is led about the stage by Mike who soon reveals that this humiliation is only part of his plan.

MIKE   . . . I want you to wait right here for me. I'm gonna go inside and get Beth. You remember her, don't ya?
(JAKE nods.)
You remember what you're gonna say to her?
(JAKE nods.)
You're not gonna forget?
(JAKE nods.)
You're gonna tell her everything that we talked about, aren't ya?
(JAKE nods.)
Good. And you're not gonna touch her. You're not gonna even think about gettin' close to her.
(JAKE shakes his head.)
Good.[109]

Having himself been earlier deemed "a dog," Mike now revels in his role as "master." This, in fact, is Mike's great flaw. Having long served as his father's whipping boy, he views existence—and, one may argue more specifically, his country[110]—as a dualistic hierarchy where one either controls or is controlled, kicks or is kicked.

Ironically, when Mike enters his home (with the flag now wrapped around his rifle) he discovers that no one is interested in his plans. Beth's concern now is not with Jake, whom she declares is "dead,"[111] but in getting Frankie well. Exasperated, Mike orders her to "forget about him"[112] (as he had earlier commanded that she forget about

Jake) and when that fails, he becomes violent. Grabbing his sister by the wrist, he struggles unsuccessfully to drag her outside. The resulting tumult awakens Baylor, who demands to know "What's goin on here?"[113] When Mike attempts to explain, Baylor, characteristically, ignores him, focussing instead on his son's gun.

> BAYLOR What're you doin with that rifle? What's that wrapped around it?
> MIKE It's just a flag. He [Jake] had it on him. He had it all wrapped around him. I wanted Beth to come out so he could—
> BAYLOR (*Pause. Taking a step toward* MIKE . . .) It's not just a flag. That's the flag of our nation. Isn't that the flag of our nation wrapped around that rifle?
> MIKE Yeah. I guess so. I don't know. I'm tryin to tell you somethin' here. The flag's not the issue.[114]

Outraged by his family's disinterest, most notably that of his father, whose world view he inherited, Mike refuses to have his crowning achievement go unrecognized. Exemplifying Jung's dictum that "where love stops, power begins, and violence,"[115] he suddenly picks Beth up and carries her screaming down the steps to Jake, whom he orders to "Get up on your feet and . . . tell her everything we talked about in the shed."[116]

Jake, however, mutinies. Rather that say what he has rehearsed, Jake tells Beth he loves her "more than this earth."[117] Here again, Shepard reveals Mike's world view to be fallacious, that one cannot control the thoughts and actions of another, no matter how much force one exerts.

Having failed in his attempt to have his family acknowledge what he has done (much less celebrate it), Mike recognizes finally that despite being the "only one who's loyal,"[118] he shall never gain his family's respect and affection.[119] Incensed by this realization, he delivers a bitterly ironic speech to Jake and then leaves for good.[120]

> Go on in there and introduce yourself. I'll bet they take you right into the family. You could use a family, couldn't ya? You look like you could use a family. Well, that's good, see. That's good. Because they could use a son. A son like you. Go ahead.[121]

After Mike's departure, Jake does, in fact, enter the house. Beth, however, does not acknowledge him as her husband, declaring instead, "Daddy, there's a man here. . . . HE'S IN OUR HOUSE!"[122] The man she once loved is now a mere stranger—a perception Jake, surprisingly, does not attempt to correct. Rather than attempt to win his wife back, he simply declares:

"Everything in me lies. But you. You stay. You are true. I know you now. You are true. I love you more than this life."[123]

In marked contrast to the man we observed at the play's beginning, who viewed his wife as an adultress, in spirit if not in deed, Jake now recognizes Beth as "true" in the broadest sense of the term, as being both faithful and having a heart, which unlike his never deceived itself. Jake then proceeds to reveal the full extent of his spiritual transformation. In an act of true contrition and selfless love, he blesses her union with the gentler, more compassionate Frankie, telling Beth, "You stay. You stay with him. He's my brother."[124]

Shortly thereafter, he gives Beth a brotherly goodbye kiss and ready, like his mother and sister, to embark upon hitherto unexplored terrain,[125] "exits upstage into darkness . . . never looking back."[126] In *A Lie of the Mind*, Jakes falls prey to his father's curse, just as the sons in *Curse of the Starving Class*, *Buried Child*, and *True West* did before him, but unlike them, he is able to transcend it. Having suffered and atoned (as best he could) for the violent things he has done, he emerges from the play a far gentler and, despite his claims to the contrary, more honest man than he had ever been before.

With Jake gone, Frankie, having consistently resisted Beth's attentions, now submits to her embrace. Long dominated by his loyalty to his brother, he appears ready at last to acknowlege the sincerity of her affections, and in so doing accept his own individuality. Furthermore, the fact that Beth and Frankie remain in this embrace for the rest of the play, suggests that this relationship, one far gentler than those we have previously seen or heard described, may last.

Meanwhile, Baylor, having been deemed unnecessary by Meg in Act Three, Scene Two, seems, as a consequence, to have had a slight change of heart as well. Once the family's autocratic martyr, a man who could complain of having to maintain a household of "crazy women" while simultaneously having his wife oil his feet, he now appears ready to serve as a somewhat more equitable partner to Meg. In an act which symbolizes this new partnership, Baylor and Meg together fold up the American flag that Mike had besmirched.[127] Moreover, once this collaboration is completed, Baylor bestows a kiss upon his wife, something he has not done for twenty years.

At the play's conclusion, Shepard again dispenses with the third wall. Meg looks out from the porch and sees Lorraine's burning bucket, which she interprets as a miracle of nature, "a fire in the snow."[128] We, however, know that what she sees is, within the context of Shepard's work, a miracle of another sort, namely a woman's liberation from a past dominated by her husband and son, from the cyclical pattern of broken hopes and familial tragedies.

In *A Lie of The Mind*, the world is not as negatively deterministic a construct as it had been in earlier father-son plays (most notably, *The Tooth of Crime*, *Curse of the Starving Class*, *Buried Child* and *True West*). Jake, Lorraine, Frankie, Sally, Beth, Meg, and, to a certain extent, Baylor have all broken free of their respective "lies of the mind," and in so doing have emancipated themselves from their pasts. Furthermore, the cold-blooded Darwinian world view, best exemplified by *The Tooth of Crime*, has been supplanted by a new and decidedly more hopeful one in which "fitness" is measured not by amoral self-interest or violent triumph but by one's capacity for cooperation, contrition, selfless love, and spiritual generosity.

Notes

1. Steven Putzel declares *A Lie of the Mind* to be a work in which audience "expectations [are] confirmed rather than confuted," and that for "those who know Shepard's previous work . . . [there is] the sense that they have seen it all before." See "Expectation, Confutation, Revelation: Audience Complicity in the Plays of Sam Shepard," *Modern Drama* 30 no.2 (June 1987), 157.

2. Ron Mottram rightly claims that "for the first time in Shepard's work [there is] a suggestion that apparently ingrained male hate and violence might be healed." See "Exhaustion of the American Soul: Sam Shepard's *A Lie of the Mind*," *Sam Shepard: A Casebook*, ed. Kimball King (New York: Garland, 1988), 98.

3. Its beginning, in fact, is nearly identical to *Curse of the Starving Class*'s conclusion. In both plays, the protagonists, realizing the inescapability of the family curse, attempt to flee their misdeeds by disappearing into barren, anonymous landscapes.

4. In Act One, Scene Three, however, he presents his motives in great detail.

5. Sam Shepard, *A Lie of the Mind* in *A Lie of the Mind and The War in Heaven*, (New York: New American Library, 1986), 2–3.

6. Ibid., 5.

7. It is via Beth's fractured declaration that Shepard introduces what will prove to be one of the play's major themes, namely the power of free will to transcend biological and familial predeterminations and effect change for the better.

8. *Lie*, 5–6.

9. It should be pointed out, however, that at this point Beth's liberation is a superficial one. True, she's escaped the dictatorial constraints of her father, but having done so she then marries a man who is equally intent on controlling her.

10. And so begins a structural pattern which pervades the whole play, whereby Shepard alternates scenes between Beth and Jake, bringing them together only for the play's denouement.

11. *Lie*, 7.

12. Ibid.

13. Ibid., 8.

14. Ibid., 11.

15. Ibid

16 Ibid., 14.

17 Ibid., 15.

18 Mottram likens Beth to the prophetess Cassandra, "the one with the clearest vision." Similarly, Janet Haedicke describes Beth's speeches as "oracular." See Mottram, "Exhaustion of the American Soul," 99, and Haedicke, "'A Population (and Theatre) at Risk'," *Modern Drama*, 36 (March 1993), 90.

19 *Lie.*, 17.

20 Ibid., 19.

21 Ibid., 18.

22 Ibid., 19.

23 Ibid., 22.

24 Lynda Hart points out, quite accurately, that by not remembering Beth's name, Lorraine is attempting to deny "Jake's transference of love-object from mother to wife." *Sam Shepard's Metaphorical Stages* (Westport, Conn: Greenwood Press, 1987), 107.

25 *Lie*, 23.

26 Ibid., 24.

27 It need be noted that never before in Shepard's work have a mother and son so resembled one another. Unlike Ella and Wesley in *The Curse of the Starving Class*, who are characterized as belonging to two altogether different species, Lorraine and Jake are psycho-spiritual dopplegangers; both self-delusive, quick to blame, violent and contentious.

28 *Lie*, 26.

29 Ibid., 27.

30 Ibid., 29–30.

31 Ibid., 31.

32 Ibid., 32.

33 Eugene O'Neill, *Long Day's Journey Into Night* (New Haven: Yale University Press, 1956).

34 Just as Lorraine does not remember who Beth is, Meg does not remember Jake. Unlike Lorraine, whose "amnesia" is motivated by the need to obliterate those whom she considers competitors for her son's heart, Meg is sincerely forgetful, and when prompted by Mike, is able to recall her son-in-law.

35 Meg, in contrast with Shepard's other mothers, does not renounce her maternal responsibilities. Unlike Ella in *Curse of the Starving Class*, who realizes her irresponsibility too late; Halie in *Buried Child*, who has always hoped that her sons, Bradley and Tilden, would take care of her; Mom in *True West*,

who vanishes in the face of a life-threatening family crisis; and Lorraine, whose reappropriation of her son, Jake, is motivated by something other than motherly concern, Meg is a true caretaker, quick to attend to the needs of her children and often childlike husband. In her character, we see but another way in which *A Lie of the Mind* deviates from the plays we have previously analyzed.

36 *Lie*, 33.

37 Ibid., 33–34.

38 Ibid., 34.

39 Like Weston in *Curse of the Starving Class* and "the old man" in *True West*, Lorraine's husband has fled the family in favor of a life alone in the desert.

40 *Lie*, 35.

41 Ibid., 36.

42 Shepard has, in essence, placed Jake atop his father's "grave" and, in so doing, subtly suggests that Jake may have played a part in his father's death.

43 *Lie*, 36.

44 Ibid., 41.

45 Ibid., 43.

46 Ibid., 44.

47 Ibid., 45.

48 Ibid., 49.

49 Ibid., 51.

50 If we look at Baylor in the context of the fathers we've previously analyzed—Man, Pop, Hoss, Weston, Dodge, and "the old man"—we will see that his relationship with his son, Mike, is marked less by ambivalence and more by pure disdain than are any of the others.

51 "'I Smash the Tools of My Captivity': The Feminine in Sam Shepard's *A Lie of the Mind*", *Rereading Shepard*, ed. Leonard Wilcox (New York: St. Martin's Press, 1993), 204.

52 "A Motel of the Mind: *Fool for Love* and *A Lie of the Mind*," *Rereading Shepard*, 220.

53 *Lie*, 46.

54 Ibid., 57.

55 Ibid.

A Lie of the Mind 103

56 Hart declares that in *A Lie of the Mind* " violence as a necessary ingredient for passionate love on the part of American men is portrayed as a lamentable truth." See *Sam hepard's Metaphorical Stages*, 109.

57 Jake is dressed, after all, like a child pretending to be his father.

58 *Lie*, 61.

59 Ibid.

60 Ibid., 61–62.

61 Ibid., 62–63

62 Ibid.

63 Ibid., 59.

64 Ibid., 67.

65 Ibid.

66 Ibid., 68.

67 Ibid.

68 Ibid., 74.

69 Ibid., 76.

70 Ibid., 76–77.

71 In a 1993 interview, Shepard reiterates this idea, stating "You know in yourself, that the female part of one's self as a man is, for the most part battered and beaten and kicked to shit just like some women in relationships . . . men themselves batter their own female part to their own detriment." See Sam Shepard, interview by Carol Rosen, "'Emotional Territory': An Interview with Sam Shepard," *Modern Drama*, 36 (March 1993), 6.

72 *Lie.*, 81.

73 Ibid.

74 "A Kind of Cavorting: Superpresence and Shepard's Family Dramas", *Rereading Shepard*, ed. Leonard Wilcox (New York: St. Martin's Press, 1993), 145.

75 *Lie*, 81

76 Ibid, 85.

77 As if to refute this claim, Shepard redirects our attention across the stage to Beth, who in the darkness screams out Jake's name. Clearly she does remember Jake, but in what context? What specifically does this cry signify? Is it one of fear or desire? Or is it a cry of grief, a recognition of having forever lost

someone whom one once loved, and, as such, a confirmation of Jake's worst fears? Shepard affords us no clues in his stage directions, preferring to keep things ambiguous until the play's last scene, when Beth is finally confronted by Jake.

78 Lorraine's collapse recalls not only that of Jake's in Act One, Scene Three, but that of Man's at the end of *The Rock Garden*. In each case, a character is literally knocked off his/her feet when confronted by the truth, which for Lorraine means that the past can neither be resurrected nor rectified.

79 *Lie*, 87.

80 Ibid., 87–88.

81 Lorraine has never asked about the actual circumstances surrounding her husband's death nor, for that matter, does she "wanna hear about that stuff now." *Lie*, 90.

82 *Lie*, 91–92.

83 Ibid., 93–94.

84 Ibid., 94–95

85 In *The Holy Ghostly*, the father's death is metaphoric and leads to his rebirth, for at the play's end, Pop himself throws a body symbolizing his own onto flames, declaring "I've never been more alive in my life, son. Never been more full a' fire and brimstone.", *The Unseen Hand and Other Plays*. 111. In *The Tooth of Crime*, Hoss takes his own life rather than suffer any further humiliation, whereas in *Buried Child*, Bradley's murderous impulses manifest themselves in comparatively benign terms, with Dodge, in the end, dying of natural causes.

86 *Lie*, 94–95.

87 Ibid. 96.

88 Ibid.

89 It is interesting to note that in *A Lie of the Mind*, collapse and convalescence serve as the prerequisites for spiritual change. Just as Beth and Jake had earlier emerged from their beds, transformed, with a new and superior awareness of themselves and the world around them, so now does Lorraine (and for that matter so shall Frankie later in the play). For a more detailed analysis of the symbolic import of Shepard's beds and blankets, see Felicia Londre, "A Motel of the Mind: *Fool for Love* and *A Lie of the Mind*," *Rereading Shepard*, 215-224.

90 *Lie*, 106.

91 Ibid.

92 "I Smash the Tools of My Captivity," 208–209.

93 *Lie*, 107.

94 In Baylor and his son, Mike, we see a masculine ethos at work where one either dominates or is dominated, or to put it in terms of the play's iconography, where one is either master or "dog." It is this narrow, dualistic world view that Shepard contests ever more actively as the play continues, until in the end Baylor capitulates (however tentatively) to the notion of cooperation, while Mike does not, leaving him no alternative but to disown the family which has already disowned him and disappear into an unspecified wilderness.

95 *Lie*, 108.

96 Ibid., 109.

97 Ibid.

98 Ibid.

99 Early in the play, Jake jealously declares that he never overlooked the fact that Frankie "always liked" Beth. *Lie*, 9.

100 It should be pointed out that Frankie is a unique character within the context of Shepard's father-son plays. Neither violent, a drunkard, nor obsessively competitive, he is the one son who appears to have altogether escaped the curse of the father. Obviously unlike Jake and Mike, the other sons in this play, Frankie somewhat resembles Boy in *The Rock Garden*, a benign character who does not actively oppose the father but rather exists simply as a contrast to him.

101 DeRose, "A Kind of Cavorting", 145.

102 "When a Woman Looks: The 'Other' Audience of Shepard's Plays," *Rereading Shepard*, 177.

103 *Lie*, 112.

104 Ibid., 114.

105 A house, we should point out, which has been as much a museum dedicated to the husband and son who abandoned her and whose return she futilely awaited (and as such, a symbol of false hope) as it was a home.

106 *Lie*, 119–120

107 The fact that Lorraine and Sally are ready, willing and able to embark upon this adventure further defines their autonomy and clearly distinguishes them from Ella, the mother in *Curse of the Starving Class*, whose plan to escape with her children to Europe is never realized and, in fact, is shot down the moment it is broached.

108 *Lie*, 120.

109 Ibid., 121–22.

110 The fact that it is an American flag which Mike uses as his reins suggests a vision of America as a Darwinian hell, where the powerful not only run roughshod over the weak, but celebrate their ability to do so.

111 *Lie*, 122.

112 Ibid.

113 Ibid., 123.

114 Ibid.

115 Carl Jung, *The Undiscovered Self*, trans. R.F.C. Hull (Boston: Little, Brown and Company, 1958), 106.

116 *Lie*, 126.

117 Ibid.

118 Ibid., 125.

119 Like Jake and Lorraine, Mike has been forced to relinquish one of his "lies." Unlike them, however, he has not been transformed, for although he concedes that, in essence, he is his family's unloved child, he never repudiates his Darwinian world view.

120 Martin Tucker claims that Mike goes off alone because he doesn't "understand his family." It may be, however, that the opposite is true, that he finally undertands his family only too well. See *Sam Shepard*, 148.

121 *Lie*, 127.

122 Ibid., 128

123 Ibid., 128–129.

124 Ibid., 129.

125 Terrain, we should point out, that is as much psycho-spiritual as it is physical.

126 *Lie*, 129.

127 It is arguable that this flag folding symbolizes more than a redefining of Meg and Baylor's relationship. Employed initially in the scene as a tool of enslavement, the flag has been transformed by the scene's end into a symbol of cooperation. By choosing to employ an American flag and in the course of the scene drastically alter its symbolic significance, Shepard moves from the microcosmic to the macrocosmic. He seems to be suggesting that America's hope lies not in an unbridled self-interest which necessitates, by its very nature, the subjugation of others, but in cooperation, forgiveness, and spiritual generosity.

128 *Lie*, 131.

Chapter Eight

Conclusion

> Sometimes I imagine the map of the world spread out and you stretched diagonally across it. And I feel as if I could consider living in only those regions that are either not covered by you or are not within your reach.[1]
> —Franz Kafka, *Letter to His Father*

Generally speaking, each of Shepard's father-son plays deal with a son's attempt to find that region that is neither "covered by . . . [nor] within [his father's] reach." In the early plays, *The Rock Garden*, *The Holy Ghostly*, and *The Tooth of Crime*, the sons succeed in extricating themselves from their fathers or father surrogates by defeating them in an Oedipal combat of some sort. In the family plays, *Curse of The Starving Class* and *Buried Child*, the sons, despite their efforts, fail to extricate themselves but rather repeat their fathers' failures. In *True West*, one son's attempt to break free of his paternal heritage results in his being punished by his father's stand-in. And in *A Lie of the Mind*, one son, Frankie, successfully escapes his father's reach, while the other, Jake, destroys the father, but is unable to escape his shadow until he assumes responsibility for what he's done and attempts a penance.

As we proceed chronologically through the first three Shepard plays analyzed, *The Rock Garden* (1964), *The Holy Ghostly* (1969), and *The Tooth of Crime* (1972), it becomes apparent that they all hold, generally speaking, to the same narrative pattern. In each play, the father or father surrogate attempts to either establish or re-establish some sort of bond with the son, is spurned, and subsequently defeated. In *The Rock Garden*, the most comic and benign of the three plays, Man imagines building a "bigger and more fancy"[2] rock garden in collaboration with Boy who, in response, falls asleep. Awaking finally at the play's end, Boy suddenly describes a recent sexual escapade in such graphic terms as to literally knock his father right out of his chair. In *The Holy Ghostly*, Pop dreams of a future where together he and Ice will "set this world on fire."³ Ice, however, shares no such dream. Intent on distinguishing himself from Pop and all that he stands for, he eventually shoots his father and walks off. In *The Tooth of Crime*, Hoss similarly extends himself, albeit in more violent terms (he is, after all, "a killer's killer"⁴). Having declared in advance of meeting Crow that he "likes this dude" and that "we might even be in the same stream,"⁵ he decides to spare him, to humiliate rather than kill him.

> Gypsy, I'm gonna whip you so bad you'll wish we had done the shivs. And then I'm gonna send you back with a mark on your forehead. *Just* a mark that won't never heal. (emphasis mine)⁶

In response, Crow accuses Hoss of misinterpreting him, of having "crossed [his] wires."⁷ Incapable of either bestowing or accepting mercy, the amoral young Gypsy is determined to fight to the death, to "lay [Hoss] out cold"⁸ and, in the end, succeeds.

Furthermore, it need be noted that as we progress from *The Rock Garden* to *The Holy Ghostly* and then to *The Tooth of Crime* the Oedipal battle between father and son grows increasingly extreme. Their conflict intensifies from a simple juxtaposition of philosophies in the first play, to a philosophical debate which resolves itself through violence in the second, to a formalized combat between two professional warriors in the third where the point from the very beginning is for each to destroy the other irrespective of their philosophical differences.

In contrast to *The Rock Garden*, *The Holy Ghostly*, and *The Tooth of Crime*, *Curse of The Starving Class* has no clear-cut winners and losers. Instead there are only predestined victims. The father, Weston, and his son, Wesley, are not adversaries. Rather, they are allies of a sort, each attempting in his own limited way to save the other from the family curse, and each ultimately failing. Initially the family's well-meaning caretaker, Wesley, by the play's last act, is as ill-kempt, violent, and impervious to reason as his drunken father. In *Curse of the Starving Class*, Shepard has created a universe that is negatively deterministic; where biology, alas, is destiny; where love has lost its power to transform; and where a family's fate is irrevocably decided at the moment of its inception.

Buried Child similarly demonstrates heredity's inescapable burden. Dodge, the father, is a drunkard and a child-murderer whose sons, Tilden and Bradley, have each in his own way followed in their father's footsteps. Having had an incestuous liaison with his mother, Tilden, like Dodge, is a breaker of taboos. He also shares his father's proclivity towards drink. Bradley, on the other hand, has inherited Dodge's capacity for violence. A veritable colossus of rage and retribution, he regularly attacks his enfeebled and defenseless old man, just as Dodge had once attacked his even more defenseless child/grandchild.

There is also a third son, Vincent, who figures prominently in the play's action. Initially unrecognized by both his father (Tilden) and his grandparents (Dodge and Halie), he leaves only to return later, drunk and violent. Having finally succumbed to the family's curse, he is now not only acknowleged but embraced, and at Dodge's death becomes the head of the household.

In contrast to *Curse of the Starving Class* and *Buried Child*, where no one wins, where the fathers and sons fall prey to the same hereditary curse, and the earlier plays where the sons defeat their fathers and thereby liberate themselves, *True West* depicts the father defeating the son (even though the former never appears on-stage). The play is essentially a revenge drama in which the father, who has been renounced, employs a surrogate to punish the son for not only having renounced him but for having flourished as a result. This surrogate is Lee, the father's violent older son and *doppleganger*,[9] while the son upon whom he seeks revenge is his younger one, Austin, a respected screenwriter with a family of his own. At the play's outset, Austin appears successfully and securely entrenched in a world beyond his father's reach. This, however, proves not to be the case. As the drama unfolds, Lee not only usurps and destroys Austin's career, but figuratively forces his younger brother out into the desert, an environment where Lee is the master and where he—and by extension his father—can exact a more permanent retribution.

In *A Lie of the Mind*, Shepard repudiates his earlier view of the world as a negatively deterministic place where sons either fall victim to a family curse from which there is no escape or remorselessly resort to violence against their fathers in order to extricate themselves. Here, for the first time, Shepard presents not only sons and fathers, but also mothers and daughters, who are capable of transcending the familial curses to which they've fallen prey. The most dramatic example of this is Jake, the play's protagonist, who has both badly beaten his wife, Beth, and murdered his drunken father. Initially incapable of accepting responsibility for either of these crimes, he is so consumed with unexpressed guilt[10] that he nearly dies. However, with the help of his sister, Sally, Jake gradually acknowledges that he, and he alone, is to blame for what he has done, and it is this realization which leads to his spiritual transformation. In what is perhaps the play's most touching moment, Jake confesses his sins to Beth. He knows now that Beth has always been "true" (in the broadest sense of the term) and that it was his and not her mind that was filled with lies. He then declares that he "loves her more than this earth"[11] and shortly thereafter demonstrates the selflessness of this love by bestowing his blessing upon Beth's and his brother, Frankie's, imminent union.

In *A Lie of the Mind*, Shepard disavows his unequivocally pessimistic world view in favor of one where gentleness, spiritual generosity, cooperation, and the acceptance of long-denied truths prevail over rage and self-interest. His protagonist, once consumed by jealousy, drunkenness, and the need to lash out, emerges from the play a gentle penitent, having transcended his father's curse through great suffering, the acknowledgement of guilt, and the subsequent making of amends.

Notes

1 Trans. Ernst Kaiser and Eithne Wilkins (New York: Shocken Books, 1966), 115.

2 *The Rock Garden*, in *Angel City and Other Plays* (New York: Urizen Books, 1976), 225.

3 *The Holy Ghostly*, in *The Unseen Hand and Other Plays* (New York: Bobbs-Merrill, 1972), 108.

4 *The Tooth of Crime*, in *The Tooth of Crime and Geography of a Horse Dreamer* (New York: Grove Press, 1974), 11.

5 Ibid., 34.

6 Ibid., 49.

7 Ibid.

8 Ibid.

9 Like his father, Lee drinks heavily, lives alone in the desert, and survives through crime and petty hustling.

10 It is this capacity for guilt (which Shepard clearly perceives as a prerequisite for change) which distinguishes Jake from Shepard's other destroyers (Ice, Crow, Bradley, Lee and Mike) who remorselessly harm others either out of revenge or self-interest.

11 *A Lie of the Mind*, in *A Lie of the Mind and The War in Heaven* (New York: New American Library, 1986), 126.

Bibliography

Aristotle. *Poetics*, trans. S.H. Butcher. New York: Hill and Wang, 1961.

Auerbach, Doris. *Sam Shepard, Arthur Kopit and Off-Broadway Theare.* Boston: Twayne, 1982.

———. "Who was Icarus's Mother?: The Powerless Mother Figures in the Plays of Sam Shepard." *Sam Shepard: A Casebook*, ed. Kimball King. New York: Garland, 1988. 53–64.

Bachman, Charles. "Defusion of Menace in the Plays of Sam Shepard." *Essays on American Drama: Williams, Miller, Albee, and Shepard*, ed. Dorothy Parker. Toronto: University of Toronto Press, 1987.

Becker, Ernest. *The Denial of Death.* New York: The Free Press, 1973.

Beckett, Samuel. *Endgame.* New York: Grove Press, 1958.

Beckson, Karl, and Arthur Ganz. *A Reader's Guide to Literary Terms.* New York: Farrar, Straus and Giroux, 1960.

Benet, Carol. *Sam Shepard on the German Stage.* New York: Peter Lang, 1993.

Bennett, Susan. "When a Woman Looks: The 'Other' Audience of Shepard's Plays." *Rereading Shepard*, ed. Leonard Wilcox. New York: St. Martin's Press, 1993. 168–179.

Bergson, Henri. *Laughter. In Comedy*, introduction by Wylie Sypher. Garden City, NY: Doubleday, 1956.

Brater, Enoch. "American Clocks: Sam Shepard's Time Plays." *Modern Drama*, 37 (Winter 1994), 603–612.

Brookhouse, Christopher. "Story Itself." *Sam Shepard: A Casebook*, ed. Kimball King. New York: Garland, 1987. 65–72.

Campbell, Joseph. *The Hero With A Thousand Faces*. Princeton, NJ: Princeton University Press, 1949.

Carroll, Dennis. "Potential Performance Texts for *The Rock Garden and 4-H Club*." *Rereading Shepard*, ed. Leonard Wilcox. New York: St. Martin's Press, 1993. 22–41.

Chaikin, Joe, and Sam Shepard. *Letters and Texts: 1972–1984*, ed. Barry Daniels. New York: New American Library, 1989.

Chubb, Kenneth. "Fruitful Difficulties of Directing Shepard." *Theatre Quarterly*, 4 (August 1974), 17–25.

Coe, Robert. "Image Shots Are Blown: The Rock Plays." *American Dreams: The Imagination of Sam Shepard*, ed. Bonnie Marranca. New York: Performing Arts Journal Publications, 1981. 57–66.

Cohn, Ruby. "Artists' Arias: Edward Bond and Sam Shepard." *Anglo-American Interplay in Recent Drama*. Cambridge: Cambridge University Press, 1995. 36–57.

———. *New American Dramatists: 1960–1980*. New York: Grove Press, 1982

———. "Sam Shepard: Today's Passionate Shepard and His Loves." *Essays on Contemporary American Drama*, ed. Hedwig Bock and Albert Wertheim. Germany: Max Hueber Verlag, 1981. 161–172.

———. "Sam Shepard." *Contemporary Dramatists*, ed. James Vinson. New York: St. Martin's Press, 1977.

Crum, Jane Ann. "'I Smash the Tools of My Captivity': The Feminine in Sam Shepard's *A Lie of the Mind*." *Rereading Shepard*, ed. Leonard Wilcox. New York: St. Martin's Press, 1993. 196–214.

———. "Notes on *Buried Child*." *Sam Shepard: A Casebook*, ed. Kimball King. New York: Garland, 1988. 73–80.

DeRose, David J. "A Kind of Cavorting: Superpresence and Shepard's Family Dramas." *Rereading Shepard*, ed. Leonard Wilcox. New York: St. Martin's Press, 1993. 131–149.

———. *Sam Shepard*. New York: Twayne, 1992.

Dugdale, John. *File on Shepard*. London: Methuen, 1989.

Falk, Florence. "Men Without Women: The Shepard Landscape." *American Dreams: The Imagination of Sam Shepard*, ed. Bonnie Marranca. New York: Performing Arts Journal Publications, 1981. 90–103.

Frazier, James. *The New Golden Bough*, ed. Theodor H. Gaster. New York: Criterion Books, 1959.

Freud, Sigmund. *Introductory Lectures on Psychoanalysis*, trans. and ed. James Strachey. New York: W.W. Norton and Co., 1966.

Frutkin, Rene. "Paired Existence Meets the Monster." *Yale/Theatre*, 2 (Summer 1969), 22–30.

Frye, Northrop. *The Anatomy of Criticism*. Princeton, NJ: Princeton University Press, 1957.

Garner, Stanton B. "Function and Physiology: Shepard's Props." *Bodied Spaces: Phenomenology and Performance in Contemporary Drama*. Ithaca: Cornell University Press, 1994. 94–103.

Geis, Deborah. "Geography of a Storyteller: Monologue in Sam Shepard's Plays." *Postmodern Theatric(k)s: Monologue in Contemporary American Drama*. Ann Arbor: University of Michigan Press, 1993. 45–88.

Gelber, Jack. "Sam Shepard: The Playwright as Shaman." *Angel City, Curse of the Starving Class & Other Plays* by Sam Shepard. New York: Urizen Books, 1976. 1–4.

Gilman, Richard. *Faith, Sex, Mystery*. New York: Simon and Schuster, 1986.

———. Introduction to *Sam Shepard: Seven Plays* by Sam Shepard. New York: Bantam Books, 1981. ix–xxv.

Grace, Sherrill. "Lighting Out for the Territory Within: Field Notes on Shepard's Expressionist Vision." *Rereading Shepard*, ed. Leonard Wilcox. New York: St. Martin's Press, 1993. 180–195.

Graham, Laura J. *Sam Shepard: Theme, Image, and the Director.* New York: Peter Lang, 1995.

Haedicke, Janet V. "'A Population (and Theatre) at Risk': Battered Women in Henley's *Crimes of the Heart* and Shepard's *A Lie of the Mind.*" *Modern Drama*, 36, (March 1993), 83–95.

Hall, Ann C. *A Kind of Alaska: Women in the Plays of O'Neill, Pinter, and Shepard.* Carbondale: Southern Illinois University Press, 1993.

Hart, Lynda. *Sam Shepard's Metaphorical Stages.* Westport, Conn: Greenwood Press, 1987.

Hayman, Ronald. *Theatre and Anti-Theatre.* New York: Oxford University Press, 1979.

Heilman, Robert B. "Shepard's Plays: Stylistic and Thematic Ties." *Sewannee Review*, 100 (Fall 1992), 630–44.

Hoeper, Jeffrey D. "Cain, Canaanites and Philistines in Sam Shepard's *True West.*" *Modern Drama*, 36 (1993), 76–82.

Holstein, Suzy C. "'All Growed Up' in the *True West*, or Huck and Tom meets Sam Shepard." *Western American Literature*, 29, no. 1 (1994), 41–50.

Jung, Carl. *The Undiscovered Self*, trans. R.F.C. Hull. Boston: Little, Brown and Co., 1958.

Kafka, Franz. *Letter to His Father*, trans. Ernst Kaiser and Eithne Wilkins. New York: Schocken Books, 1966.

Kauffmann, Stanley. "What Price Freedom?" *American Dreams: The Imagination of Sam Shepard*, ed. Bonnie Marranca. New York: Performing Arts Journal Publications, 1981. 104–107.

———. *Persons of the Drama.* New York: Harper and Row, 1976.

King, Kimball, ed. *Sam Shepard: A Casebook.* New York: Garland, 1988.

Kleb, William. "Worse Than Being Homeless: True West and The Divided Self." *American Dreams: The Imagination of Sam Shepard*, ed. Bonnie Marranca. New York: Performing Arts Journal Publications, 1981. 117–125.

Kroll, Jack. "Who's That Tall Dark Stranger?" *Newsweek*, 11 November 1985, 68–74.

Lahr, John and Jonathan Price, eds. *The Great American Life Show: 9 Plays From the Avant-Garde Theatre*. New York: Bantam Books, 1974.

Lanier, Gregory. "Two Opposite Animals: Structural Pairings in Sam Shepard's *A Lie of the Mind*." *Modern Drama*, 34 (September 1991), 410–21.

———. "The Killer's Ancient Mask: Unity and Dualism in Shepard's *The Tooth of Crime*." *Modern Drama*, 36 (March 1993), 48–60.

Londre, Felicia Harison. "A Motel of the Mind: *Fool for Love* and *A Lie of the Mind*." Rereading Shepard, ed. Leonard Wilcox. New York: St. Martin's Press, 1993.

Lion, John. "Rock and Roll Jesus with a Cowboy Mouth: Sam Shepard is the Inkblot of the '80s." *American Theatre*, 1, no. 1 (April 1984), 4–13.

Lyons, Charles R. "Shepard's Family Trilogy and the Conventions of Modern Realism." *Rereading Shepard*, ed. Leonard Wilcox. New York: St. Martin's Press, 1993. 115–130.

Mann, Bruce J. "Character Behavior and the Fantastic in Sam Shepard's *Buried Child*." *Sam Shepard: A Casebook*, ed. Kimball King. New York: Garland Publishing, 1988. 81–94.

Marcuse, Herbert. "Varieties of Humanism." *Center Magazine*, June 1968, 14.

Marranca, Bonnie. "Alphabetical Shepard: A Play of Words." *American Dreams: The Imagination of Sam Shepard*. New York: Performing Arts Journal Press, 1981. 13–33.

———, ed. *American Dreams: The Imagination of Sam Shepard*. New York: Performing Arts Journal Press, 1981.

———, and Gautam Dasgupta, eds. *American Playwrights: A Critical Survey*. Vol. 1. New York: Drama Book Specialists, 1981.

McDonough, Carla J. "The Politics of Stage Space: Women and Male Identity in Sam Shepard's Family Plays." *Journal of Dramatic Theory and Criticism* 9, no. 2 (1995), 65–83.

McGhee, Jim. *True Lies: The Architecture of the Fantastic in the Plays of Sam Shepard.* New York: Peter Lang, 1993.

Mottram, Ron. "Exhaustion of the American Soul: Sam Shepard's *A Lie of the Mind.*" *Sam Shepard: A Casebook,* ed. Kimball King. New York: Garland, 1988. 95–106.

———. *Inner Landscapes: The Theatre of Sam Shepard.* Columbia: University of Missouri Press, 1984.

Nash, Thomas. "Sam Shepard's *Buried Child*: The Ironic Use of Folklore." *Essays on American Drama: Williams, Miller, Albee, and Shepard,* ed. Dorothy Parker. Toronto: University of Toronto Press, 1987.

Nietzsche, Friedrich. *The Birth of Tragedy* and *The Genealogy of Morals,* trans. Francis Golffing. Garden City, NY: Doubleday Anchor Books, 1956.

Nightingale, Benedict. "Even Minimal Shepard is Food for Thought," *New York Times,* 25 September 1983, sec. 2, p. 5.

O'Neill, Eugene. *Long Day's Journey Into Night.* New Haven: Yale University Press, 1956.

Orbison, Tucker. "Mythic Levels in Shepard's True West." *Essays on American Drama: Williams, Miller, Albee, and Shepard,* ed. Dorothy Parker. Toronto: University of Toronto Press, 1987.

Orr, John. *Tragicomedy and Contemporary Culture: Play and Performance from Beckett to Shepard.* Hampshire: Macmillan, 1991.

Oumano, Ellen. *Sam Shepard: The Life and Work of an American Dreamer.* New York: St. Martin's Press, 1986.

Parker, Dorothy, ed. *Essays on American Drama: Williams, Miller, Albee, and Shepard.* Toronto: University of Toronto Press, 1987.

Patraka, Vivian M., and Marc Siegel. *Sam Shepard.* Boise: Boise State University Press, 1985.

Perry, Frederick J. *A Reconstruction Analysis of Buried Child by Playwright Sam Shepard.* San Francisco: Mellen Research University Press, 1992.

Poland, Albert, and Bruce Mailman, eds. *The Off-Off Broadway Book: The Plays, People, Theatre.* New York: Bobbs-Merrill, 1972.

Powe, Bruce W. "*The Tooth of Crime:* Shepard's Way with Music." *Essays on American Drama: Williams, Miller, Albee, and Shepard*, ed. Dorothy Parker. Toronto: University of Toronto Press, 1987.

Putzel, Steven. "Expectation, Confutation, Revelation: Audience Complicity in the Plays of Sam Shepard." *Modern Drama*, 30, no. 2. (June 1987) 147–160.

Rabillard, Sheila. "Shepard's Challenge to the Modernist Myths of Origin and Originality: *Angel City* and *True West.*" *Rereading Shepard*, ed. Leonard Wilcox. New York: St. Martin's Press, 1993. 77–96.

Randall, Phyllis R. "Adapting to Reality: Language in Shepard's *Curse of the Starving Class.*" *Sam Shepard: A Casebook*, ed. Kimball King. New York: Garland, 1988. 121–134.

Robinson, Marc. "Sam Shepard." *The Other American Drama*. Cambridge: Cambridge University Press, 1994. 60–88.

Rozak, Theodore. *The Making of a Counter Culture.* Garden City, NY: Doubleday, 1969.

Schechner, Richard. "The Writer and the Performance Group: Rehearsing *The Tooth of Crime.*" *American Dreams: The Imagination of Sam Shepard*, ed. Bonnie Marranca. New York: Performing Arts Journal Publications, 1981. 162–170.

Schroeder, Robert J., ed. *The New Underground Theatre.* New York: Bantam, 1968.

Schvey, Henry I. "Worm in the Wood: The Father-Son Relationship in the Plays of Sam Shepard." *Modern Drama*, 36 (March 1993), 12–25.

Shepard, Sam. *Cruising Paradise: Tales by Sam Shepard.* New York: Knopf, 1996.

———. "Emotional Territory: An Interview with Sam Shepard." Interview by Carol Rosen. *Modern Drama*, 36 (March 1993), 1–11.

———. *States of Shock, Far North, Silent Tongue*. New York: Vintage Books, 1993.

———. *A Lie of the Mind*. In *A Lie of the Mind and The War in Heaven*. New York: New American Library, 1986.

———. "Rhythm and Truth: An Interview with Sam Shepard." Interview by Amy Lippman. *American Theatre* 1, no. 1 (1984).

———. *Motel Chronicles*. San Francisco: City Lights, 1982.

———. *True West*. Garden City, NY: Doubleday, 1981.

———. *Chicago and Other Plays*. New York: Urizen Books, 1981.

———. *Hawk Moon*. New York: Performing Arts Journal Publications, 1981.

———. *Buried Child*. In *Buried Child, Seduced, Suicide in B Flat*. New York: Urizen Books, 1979.

———. "Visualization, Language, and the Inner Library." *Drama Review*, 21, no. 4 (December 1977), 49–58.

———. *Curse of the Starving Class*. In *Angel City, Curse of the Starving Class & and Other Plays*. New York: Urizen Books, 1976.

———. *The Rock Garden*. In *Angel City, Curse of the Starving Class & Other Plays*. New York: Urizen Books, 1976.

———. *The Tooth Of Crime*. In *The Tooth of Crime and Geography of a Horse Dreamer*. New York: Grove Press, 1974.

———. *The Holy Ghostly*. In *The Unseen Hand and Other Plays*. New York: Bobbs-Merrill, 1972

———. *Mad Dog Blues and Other Plays*. New York: Winter House LTD, 1972.

———. *La Turista*. New York: Bobbs-Merrill, 1968.

Shewey, Don. *Sam Shepard*. New York: Dell, 1985.

Smith, Michael, ed. *The Best of Off-Off Broadway*. New York: Dutton Books, 1969.

Sparr, Landy, Susan Erstling and James Boehnlein. "Sam Shepard and the Dysfunctional Family: A Therapeutic Perspective." *American Journal of Psychotherapy*, 44 (October 1990), 563–76.

Todorov, Tzvetan. *The Fantastic: A Structural Approach to a Literary Genre*. Ithaca, NY: Cornell University Press, 1975.

Tucker, Martin. *Sam Shepard*. New York: Continuum, 1992.

Weales, Gerald. "Artifacts: The Early Plays Reconsiderd." *Rereading Shepard*, ed. Leonard Wilcox. New York: St. Martin's Press, 1993. 8–21.

Wilcox, Leonard, ed. *Rereading Shepard*. New York: St. Martin's Press, 1993.

Wilson, Ann. "True Stories: Reading the Autobiographic in *Cowboy Mouth, True Dylan and Buried Child*." *Rereading Shepard*, ed. Leonard Wilcox. New York: St. Martin's Press, 1993. 97–114.

Wren, Scott Christopher. "Camp Shepard: Exploring the Geography of Character." *West Coast Plays*, vol. 7 (Fall 1980), 73–106.